VICTOR PACINI
WINNING WITHIN

Impossible life events with "I'm Possible" results

Never Give Up!

Victor

2019

Editor: Bill Dal Cerro
Cover Design & Layout: The VIC Design Team

Winning Within - (Impossible Life Events with I'm Possible Results)
by Victor Pacini. --3rd. ed. ISBN: 978-0-9740233-1-1

ISBN: 978-0-9740233-1-1
Printed in the U.S.A.

DEDICATIONS

To Mimmi, Angelo, and Luca:
It is my intention to teach you
to live life fully. I have learned that
because of you, I am fully alive.
I am honored to be your dad.
I love you.

CONTENTS

INTRODUCTION

I was named Victor after my grandfather on my mother's side. One day, I looked up my name in a dictionary. It said that the word victor means "a person who has overcome or defeated an adversary; conqueror, and a winner in any struggle or contest." I thought that was interesting but didn't think much about it. As a young boy, my friends and family called me Vic, so I pretty much put my official name on hold and went with a nickname. As I got older, people began calling me names like Vince and Nick. I really didn't know why except people told me that I looked like a Vince. What does that mean? I constantly would correct them but I stopped after a while because it happened so frequently. I worked at a grocery store in high school and my manager called me Nick many times--which was funny, since all he had to do was look at my name tag.

The older I became, the more I decided to go back to my official name. After all, my grandfather would be proud, even though I never met him. It is fitting to share this with you because the meaning of my name has led me on a journey for the last 15 years of my life. Let me preface this journey with my definition of the word victor. I love to compete at sports. When I was on the high school baseball team, I loved to play and win. However, this book talks about a different kind of victor or victory. Best-selling author, Dr. Wayne Dyer inspired me with his definition of True Nobility: "It's not about being better than anyone else. It's about being better than you used to be."

To me, that's the most important victory of all. So I ask: Do you feel like a winner in your life? What would you say? I say, life is a work in progress! My promise to myself is to be better than I used to be. This leads me to the purpose of this book. I know that obstacles or adversities (whatever you want to call them) make us better people as a result of those obstacles or struggles. That's assuming you can transcend the obstacles and learn from them. I know so many people who use their past obstacles as reasons for their current state of unhappiness. But I take responsibility for me. No one really can bring me down without my allowing it to happen. I also take responsibility for the obstacles. Whether I caused them or they were done to me, I take responsibility for using them as an opportunity to grow and expand internally. To me, that's true nobility!

When I speak to teens and adults, I ask them to imagine their eyeballs as the most sophisticated cameras in the world. With these eyeballs you can scan situations and ultimately make choices based on your assessments. These choices can lead you to something with a good outcome or a bad one, but nonetheless, you have to make that choice. Dr. Wayne Dyer said, "You are doomed to make choices." It's like going to a party: You scan left and see negative behavior, i.e. drugs, drinking, or people putting others down; or you look right and you see positive behavior.

It's up to you alone to decide what you want. I believe you have the choice to be the director, producer, writer, and actor or actress of your own movie called Life. Sometimes you go about your life being the director and something happens without your control. You have two choices: You can grow from it or not. This sounds black and white, but most of the time we suffer for long periods of time before we go from asking, Why? to asking What can I do with this? Things happen that make us sad, angry, and frustrated. I have learned that things happen and it's our reaction to those things that give us these emotions. Best-selling author and speaker Dr. Leo Buscaglia said, "There are two big forces at work, external and internal. We have very little control over external forces such as tornadoes, earthquakes, floods, disasters, illness and pain. What really matters is the internal force. How do I respond to those disasters? Over that I have complete control."

I think the key is to get to a place inside of you that speeds up the process of not suffering for long periods of time. Best-selling author and founder of the revolutionary process called "The Work", Byron Katie calls these emotions "the temple bells that tell you to go within." Once you go in and learn from the situation and take responsibility, the faster you enjoy your life at higher levels. You have to learn to be more in the present and not stay stuck in the past.

It is my intention with this book to share some of my most personal life experiences, which caused me to be the person I am today. Everything happens for a reason. I may not know the reason but it happens. That's the way it is! Please understand that I don't have the answers for you. Only you can discover the answers for yourself. I can maybe open some doors for you but you have to decide to walk through and create a wonderful life. I am not even asking you to walk through any door. All I ask you to do is open your mind enough to know that there are doors for you to explore.

I recently watched "Monsters, Inc" with my daughter. This has become one of my favorite movies. The basic idea is that the monsters have a job to scare children. They come out of the children's closets and into their bedrooms. Their job is to get the most screams. The more they get kids to scream, the more energy is produced for the city called Monstropolis. One day, a monster realizes that the children's laughs can create even more energy than the screams. This monster understands that by having an open mind it can create similar results without causing so much fear. It's all because of an open mind that new ideas materialize and, ultimately, new doors open. It is my hope that your mind stays open.

With gratitude,

Victor

(P.S. You can call me Vince.)

OVERCOME THE SKATEBOARD

"In the middle of every obstacle lies opportunity."
~Albert Einstein

I am fascinated with the concept of dreams. When I was a little boy, no one ever really asked me what I wanted to be when I grew up. I think children should have dreams and I think adults should never stop dreaming. I think children should dream about the impossible. Why not? Just think, before electricity, no one thought it could exist until Benjamin Franklin and others came along with an open mind. People were skeptical about the idea of men and women flying. The Wright Brothers changed that. I can go on and on. Dr. Wayne Dyer said, "No one knows enough to be a pessimist." That's a great way to look at it. If you know a child, encourage them to dream and think of all of the possibilities.

I was inspiring children at a school not too long ago when I asked a boy what he wanted to be when he got older. He said, "When I grow up I want to be a professional skateboarder." I said, "That's so cool." I went further with the questioning: "When you are on your board, do you ever fall off?" He laughed, "All of the time!" Then I asked, "So, when you fall off do you just lay there and wait for someone to come get you?" He said, "No! I get up, dust myself off and get back on my skateboard and keep going." That boy was so wise.

Whenever I am in front of children I always go in with the mindset that I can learn just as much from them as they can learn from me. It's so true. To me, this boy knew the secret to an incredible life. You are going to fall off your skateboard. Things are going to happen that will hurt. But, to move on with your life, you have to get up and keep going. I call this **overcoming the skateboard**.

Some people try to avoid the skateboard altogether. They feel safer that way. They refuse to take risks. They refuse to try. Out of fear, they avoid living life with all of its wonder and opportunities. A flower that stops growing dies. You have to grow. Growing means to experience and allow your life to unfold as it will. It comes down to a choice. One, you can feel sorry for yourself. If that's the case, you will continue to attract more of those negative feelings. You will attract people who will feel sorry for you. You will continue to grow into someone who lives a sorry life. Or, two, you can take the risk to fall and get up yet be willing to fall again. Life happens and it's up to you to pick yourself up. The initial action has to come from you.

I have a friend whom I met 12 years ago. At the time, she was shy and introverted. One day, I showed her some designs that I created which depicted one of my personal obstacles. I created these designs for a school project. I always designed from my personal experiences because it was a kind of therapy for me. It was always something I was passionate about so it came out with the work I produced. I guess seeing my work opened a door for my friend. She felt comfortable with our relationship and shared her story with me of being repeatedly abused as a child. Getting it off her chest was an epiphany for her. She later came to one of my performances and was so thankful for helping her see the light. I honestly told her I did nothing to help her. She thanked me again and said I was the reason for her healing and her ability to overcome the skateboard. I told her again it wasn't me. You have to make the decision to create whatever changes you want for your life.

I am so grateful that my friend has made positive changes in her life. She's not afraid anymore. She lives life with a passion, confidence and energy about herself that has taken her to new levels, personally and professionally. She loves to dance. She loves to talk to people. I love her for that. I love that she is in a happier place in her life. She deserves it and SO DO YOU!

I have longed listened to motivational CD's and read inspirational books. Dr. Wayne Dyer, Dr. Leo Buscaglia, Byron Katie and Dan Millman are some of my favorite authors. I have learned so much from them. They have been my teachers on many levels. I bet they would agree with me that they put their ideas out there in a way that worked for them but that it was up to me to use them or not. I know they never take credit for someone's healing or ability to find love. I, too, never take credit for someone's "Ah ha!" moments.

My passion is to share my story and hope that it will resonate with you. Here's a quick example: Imagine a buffet. All this wonderful food waits for you. No one will get it for you. You must get up and go see the choices that are available, then chose.

I close this chapter with a quote from Dan Sullivan and Catherine Nomura's The Laws of Lifetime Growth:
"The biggest challenge to leaving our comfort zone is always fear: fear that we'll fail, fear that someone will discover that we're not as good as they thought we were, fear that we'll lose something important, fear that people won't understand what we're doing-the list goes on and on. Confidence is the ability to transform these fears into focused thinking and action."

Confidence is what you need to get back up on that skateboard so you can ride and ride and ride.

THE CAMEL

"You must do the things you think you cannot do."
~Eleanor Roosevelt

As I said previously, I refer to my healing of any negative situation in my life as overcoming the skateboard. I like to keep that very wise comment by that 4th grader in my mind as I write this book. See, when we get older we have a tendency to be the teacher for others. It's important to keep in perspective that some of the wisest people can be young children. Never stop learning! Learning leads to growing and we already know that a flower that doesn't grow doesn't live.

I was born on January 30, 1972 in Chicago, IL. I am the youngest of five children. My mom was a stay-at-home mom with a passion for her family. She eventually went back to work after my father suffered his fourth heart attack and couldn't work any longer. In the early days, my father owned a gas station and later a successful towing business for over twenty-five years. He worked hard to provide for us.

From left to right:
Michele, Victor, Grandma (Nonni), Angelo, Reneé, and Laura (Taken around 1974)

On August 16, 1977, our family moved from Chicago to Mt. Prospect. Ironically this was the same day that Elvis Presley died. (I will explain the importance of that later on.) I remember my family being pretty close. My brother was eight years older than me. There were times I felt like a boy who didn't fit in because all my siblings had their own lives. This doesn't mean they didn't care about me. I was loved by all. I was the baby. There is something about being the youngest. I think it's pretty amazing because you get to see what everyone is doing and then you do the complete opposite! That's not totally true. In fact, it's great to be the youngest because you can learn so much from the older ones. I recall a special connection to my oldest sister, Michele. She was kind of my second mom when my mother was taking care of the camel. Well, he wasn't a camel yet. (I will explain the camel at the end of the chapter.) He was more like Dr. Jekyll and Mr. Hyde. One minute he was my dad and the next he was a monster.

As a child, you go off to bed at night hoping to dream of wonderful places and incredible experiences. Nightmares can be uncomfortable, especially for children. I actually had those from time to time. But the nightmares I am talking about are those waking nightmares. I would wake up in the middle of the night to the sounds of screams, objects breaking, and the sound of skin being hit. My father was no longer my father but the monster I was talking about. As a young child I noticed that he only became this monster when he drank a liquid called alcohol. This liquid transformed him into a violent person.

Even his facial features changed. He looked really angry and ready to take on anyone who came in his path. It looked as though he was waiting for a fight. As a family we wouldn't talk about it. It's like when something breaks and instead of picking it up you sweep it under the carpet, hoping that no one walks over it and discovers it. This was how we dealt with my dad's drinking problem.

This problem became an even bigger problem because we were being taught to suppress our feelings, our confusion, and, ultimately, a part of ourselves. I can't put into words how my siblings and I felt when the monster would appear. Even as I write this, I feel my heart pounding faster and faster. It was a very scary time for me personally. I can't imagine what it was like for the ones who met him head on. I will never forget a time he was so intoxicated that he took a rifle out and began walking around the house. We became hostages in our own home. My sister called the police and within minutes our house was surrounded. My father finally released the rifle after truly scaring everyone around him.

I will never forget the breakfast mornings I had with my dad. While I ate my breakfast, he drank his. I recall smoke hovering overhead from his cigarettes as I ate my Count Chocula Cereal. My father would get up and walk to the pantry and pick out his drink of choice, take a swig, and sit back down. He did this numerous times. That visual has never left my mind. It's funny, but otherwise my life seemed pretty normal overall. I guess the key word in this case is "seemed".

I recall a day when my whole family, including my dog, picked me up from school. At first, I was so happy to see them. Then I realized that we were leaving my dad again. We had to get away. He was out of control again. We stayed at my aunt and uncle's house in Elmwood Park. These visits usually lasted two days. It was inevitable, though, we eventually went home to face this monster.

I will never forget one time when we entered the house, I can vividly remember my father sitting on the couch with cigarette in hand. The smoke was rising along with his temper. The ashtray filled to the brim with cigarette butts. The fuel for the monster sat next to him in a glass, staring at him and waiting to be picked up. I think it was some kind of whisky but no one ever really knew. It got to the point where he would drink anything that had alcohol, including mouth wash. I remember going up to him and telling him that I loved him, but he told me to get out of his face. It's not that he didn't want to see me, on the contrary, it's that he didn't want me to see him so low. I know that now, but at the time I was very upset. In life, when someone tells you something that comes across mean or crude, it's not you, it's the person who has the issue. The Buddha once said "When someone offers you a gift and you refuse to accept that gift, to whom does the gift belong"? When someone wants to put you down you have to know that it's not you; it's the person who is doing the yelling. Don't accept that gift or that anger. The gift has to be returned to the sender.

Once again, we shoved every incident under the carpet and didn't talk about it. That's what we were expected to do. You never questioned it. You never asked why. You were expected to move along and go to school and learn math and science. The problem is that you then hold that stuff inside and it festers into all kinds of things. I now know that everything is energy. There's high and low levels of energy. By holding all of this low energy inside of you, it takes a toll and eventually catches up to you.

In 1980, I was diagnosed with asthma. I was running at school one day and I had an attack. My life became somewhat challenged because of this "disease." Now that I think back was it a disease or was it brought on because of the stuff under the rug? I do know that asthma is a real condition but is it possible that stressful thoughts can cause the asthma to become stronger? I think so. As I got older and we had family parties where alcohol was available, I always seemed to have a severe asthma attack. I was afraid that my dad was going to start with his rampage again so I allowed that stress to get to me and that brought on an asthma attack. I was rushed to a hospital where I could be treated and taken care of. There was no smoking or drinking at the hospital. There was no yelling or attacking. There were people there waiting to help me with what was bothering me. They were there to treat my asthma attack. I don't think asthma actually attacks. I think negative thoughts attack. I think stress attacks. I think intoxicated people attack. I think dads hitting moms attack our inner body of perfect health. When this body of perfect health is threatened, it breaks down and we have ulcers, asthma attacks, heart attacks, and anxiety attacks.

There is a happy ending to this story: My dad admitted his problem. That was a huge breakthrough. The first time he tried to quit, he relapsed. The second time he tried, he was successful and has been for over 28 years.

At the beginning of the chapter, I called my father a camel. I learned this from my mentor, Dr. Wayne Dyer. I adopted this term for my dad. A camel is an animal that goes to bed every night on its knees. It wakes up every morning on its knees, and goes twenty-four hours without a drink. My dad goes twenty-four hours without a sip of alcohol...one day at a time. I am so proud of him. Here's a man who has these addictive behaviors and was able to see that he didn't need alcohol any longer. He knows he is a better person because of it. That's an amazing example of True Nobility.

Here's how to **Overcome The Skateboard:**

I was frustrated, sad, and angry with my father for causing such pain to the family. I was so saddened by the way he hurt my mom over and over again. I overcame by forgiving him. This is an essential key to this whole book. Mark Twain said it perfectly, "Forgiveness is the fragrance the violet sheds on the heel that has crushed it." Please read this over and over. I had to do so many times to truly understand it. I forgave my father because he helped himself to become a better person. If you don't forgive, then you physically live today while your mind is living in the past. We all know that the past is the past. You can't change it. You can use it either to complain or sustain. If you complain about it, it's because you have not forgiven someone or even yourself for that matter. For you to live a full life, you must forgive that person who has hurt you. Forgiveness is the only way to Overcome The Skateboard.

I am not saying that you still have to be in contact with that person. In this case, I forgave and wanted to continue my relationship with my father. I am grateful to have the time with him today. My father taught me something that even my personal heroes in my life could never teach me. He taught me what not to do. He is one of my greatest teachers. I now have two children and my dad taught me not to treat them like he treated my siblings and myself. I will never become an alcoholic. Why? I have made a conscious choice to not go down that path. My dad's behavior opened a door for me--a door that I willingly slammed shut.

Another way I Overcame The Skateboard was to take the pain and use it as a topic for my artwork in college. I got to a place where I was comfortable depicting images that showed my courage. I was also able to let go of my past and not allow it to run my life in the present moment. In a book titled 10 Secrets for Success and Inner Peace by Dr. Wayne Dyer, he explains your past in these terms: "When a speedboat zooms across the surface of the water, there's a white foamy froth behind it called the wake of the boat. The wake is nothing more than a trail that's left behind. The answer to "What's driving the boat?" is that the boat moves because of the present moment energy generated by the engine. This is what makes the boat move forward across the water. Do you think it's possible for the wake to drive the boat? Can the trail that's left behind make the boat go forward? These are rhetorical questions with obvious answers. I am suggesting that you apply this idea to your life. The wake of your life is nothing more than a trail that's left behind you. Thought of in this way, it's absolutely impossible for the wake to drive you forward."

He then goes on saying, "The wake is just what it is, and nothing more-a trail that you've left behind." You can't live in the wake of your life. I believe you can use those "wake" memories as teachers of the true insights into your life.

I love my father more now than ever. Forgiveness is a very high energy. My suggestion to you is to forgive the person who has hurt you. When you do, you will live more in the present. You will be able to focus more on your work and play. There is an expression which says that "yesterday is history, tomorrow is a mystery, and today is a gift....that's why they call it the present." Forgiveness is a present that is waiting for you to rip open so you can check out the possibilities to live in the present everyday.

Common memories during my childhood · Drawing/Computer · Harper College · 1993

Passed out in the bathroom. Charcoal Pencil Drawing · Harper College · 1993

SCROOGE IS ON TV AGAIN

*"Without Darkness nothing comes to birth,
As without light nothing flowers."*
~May Sarton, American Poet & Novelist

Elvis Presley died on August 16, 1977. Ironically, this was the day the Pacini Family moved to Mt. Prospect. I can recall my family, and especially my brother, being very upset. As a five year old, I didn't understand what was going on at the time. Who would have thought that a famous man I knew little about would become such an important person in my life?

My brother Angelo is one of my personal heroes. He is truly a gentle man with a very loving heart. I love him and Angelo loves Elvis. He began collecting Elvis music right around the time of the move. My dad bought a Jukebox and Angelo filled it up with Elvis music. One day, don't ask me why, I began listening and singing to these songs. I can't explain why I was so attracted to this kind of music, or why I even began doing it in the first place. Needless to say, I began to shake my leg and curl my lip. Elvis was known for his crazy moves on stage. He actually was censored on many TV stations because he was considered vulgar and obscene. I believe he was creating something so new that people were not used to this type of change. To me, that's genius.

My Elvis act got to the point that I would perform it for the family. It was weird. How many eight-year-old boys do you know who dress up like Elvis and sing in front of thousands of people? My father knew of a Tribute to Elvis Band that was looking for a "little Elvis". I found enough courage and tried out. I became the warm up act for the main event. My stage name was Master Vic. I toured with the show for four years. My weekend trips took me to New York, Michigan, Arkansas, and many other states.

With this type of life style, I was around many people. My parents were very trusting people. I met this woman who had a son. He was much older than me. One day, my parents let me spend the night with his family. While he and I were in his room, he sexually abused me. After he stopped, he wanted me to reciprocate. As I look back, I am very proud of myself because I knew at that time that it was wrong. I will never forget that day. The old black and white version of the movie *Scrooge* was on the television. I am so grateful that it only happened once. He told me I better not tell my parents because they would be very angry with me. I didn't tell a soul. I stored it in a very dark place in my mind. I wanted to forget that it even hap-pened. It was a problem because Christmas came every year. That movie *Scrooge* was shown numerous times. When I came across it, I immediately went back to that moment. It's amazing how we associate things with what we see, hear, or taste to an experience in our past.

Still, I kept the abuse a secret for 9 years. I can truly say there were times I didn't think about it and my life went forward. There were times I did think about it and my life went on but with sadness, tears, and confusion. As I began high school, I questioned my sexuality. Since my first sexual experience was with a male, I had these questions in my mind. It didn't take long for me to realize that it was just my stressful thinking, and I soon knew who I was in that department. I remember being attracted to girls in high school but because I was shy, I didn't do anything about it. I didn't even go to my prom.

What I was really struggling with was the idea of not dealing with the abuse. I was victimized and I didn't know how to deal with it. I recall taking psychology in high school and the topic of deviant behavior came up on many occasions. In my mind, I went right back to that bedroom with *Scrooge* on TV. I began the realization that I was pushed off my skateboard and that my thoughts kept me on the ground. I felt paralyzed and helpless. I couldn't undo the fact but I knew I would do something about getting on that skateboard again.

My breakthrough happened in the summer of 1990. I entered my first year at Millikin University that August. After one month of living away from home, I broke down one day in my dorm room. My grades were just OK and I was struggling. I had just finished high school in the top

5% in my class but I couldn't seem to focus on school. Then it hit me: I was sexually abused and it was time to get help. You see, once you decide to get back on the skateboard, then and only then will people show up to help you. I needed to tell someone. I called home and my sister Reneé answered the phone. She couldn't understand why I sounded so strange. I couldn't say the words. I was vague in my description. I was ashamed. After asking me many questions, Reneé began to see that I was in pain and something was wrong. I left school immediately and began my healing. This was my life, and I couldn't go further with my education until I dealt with this fall.

I went to a place called Northwest Action Against Rape. I met with a wonderful young lady who was there for me. What was so amazing about her was that she wasn't so interested in knowing the particulars of the abuse. She wanted me to come to terms with it and be able to open up at my level of comfort. Admitting that it happened was one step closer to healing. She was so amazing. Being able to admit and say I was abused was the momentum I needed to get back on the skateboard and be free once again.

Here's how to **Overcome The Skateboard:**

Because I am a visual person, I once again used the source of my pain in my artwork in school. This became a vehicle to my healing.

Up to this point in my life, this abuse was the most devastating obstacle. I forgave this person; however, this is a situation where I forgave from a distance. There was no need for confrontation. There was no need for any type of communication. I just went in and forgave from the heart. That's what is so great about forgiveness. It's not for anyone else. Because I didn't want to have contact with this person I used forgiveness for myself. Forgiveness is actually one word and two words. There's "forgiving" and "for giving." I gave this present to me, from me. If there is something going on right now with you, my suggestion is to find that someone you can trust and then begin your healing.

PSA For Advertising Class • Columbia College • 1995
This was my way of depicting my transformation from victim to survivor.
I was the designer and photographer for this piece.

Master Vic's first promo picture • 1980

THANK YOU FOR SPENDING YOUR TIME THINKING ABOUT ME.

"The pessimist sees difficulty in every opportunity.
The optimist sees the opportunity in every difficulty."
~Winston Churchill

Admitting and sharing my abuse made me a stronger more focused individual. This allowed for a personal transformation that took place in my early to mid twenties. It was such an amazing time for me. One thing I began to question was, Why I am here? What's the real point to life? I began to read books on Zen Philosophy, self-improvement, and selections from one of my all time favorites, Dr. Leo Buscaglia. I loved to find ways in which I could improve my life. I wanted to live at higher levels of consciousness. What can I do to be happy most of the time? There were many nights I would go to Starbucks on my way to perform at a local club and sit down with a latté and read. These were probably some of the most "present moment" experiences in my life. I just sat and read alone. One night, I came across an ad for a Buddhist Monastery in Mt. Shasta, California. I was very intrigued. I decided to see how the monks lived. It was a pretty crazy idea but for me it was something that was calling me. I wanted to learn how to meditate. I made my plane reservations, rented a car, and told my parents. My mother protested because she thought it was a cult and I would never come home. I wrote a letter to them before I left, reassuring them I would only be gone for a week. It was a freeing experience because I had never done anything like this before. It was an adventure! I was ready to try something different with my life.

I rented a car when I arrived in Redding (about 60 miles south of Mt. Shasta.) It was eighty degrees when I started my journey. By the time I reached the monks the temperature dropped to thirty degrees. Here was a monastery surrounded by trees and mountains. The mountains welcomed me as I drove in-between the rocks and so, too, did the monks, with open arms, as if I was a long-lost relative. They taught me mindfulness. When you eat, eat. You don't think about dessert while you are eating your main course. You don't think about the next day. You live moment to moment. They taught me how to do working meditation. I had a job putting labels on some mailers for the monastery. That was my job. I was to do it without thinking about anything else. It's interesting because in our culture we have been taught that "on the go" is the way to go. We move too fast.

I loved it there. I meditated with the monks and talked to them about life. As my visit moved forward, they began to really dive into the religious aspect of Zen. Even though I am respectful of all religions, I wasn't there to learn about the religion as much as the philosophy. I cut my trip short and called home to tell my parents I was coming home early. My mom was thrilled.

The experience itself was the lesson I was seeking. I flew to San Francisco, jumped on another small plane and flew to Redding, California. I share this with you because I think it's great to experience life in different and creative ways. If something is in your heart that you want to experience one day you should consider it. I will say that I didn't need to go far away to find happiness or contentment. I didn't have to go far at all. It was right under my nose. However, I wouldn't have traded the experience for anything.

I share the Mt. Shasta experience because I believe it helped me get past this next hurdle. It helped me realize the difference between reacting to situations and understanding them for what they are. When you react you are letting the situation get the best of you. When you are allowing a situation to unfold without anger, you are demonstrating peace and control. Let's just say that the peace that the monks taught me guided me to overcome the next skateboard of my life.

Remember earlier when I told you about the Elvis tribute band I worked with when I was a child? The main performer in that band was and still is a very talented singer. If I ever had an idol it was this person because I wanted to be like him. I marveled at what he did on stage but as I grew up, he grew into someone who wasn't always supportive of my career. In fact, he probably didn't think I would last in this profession. What I have learned as a performer is that when you are on stage you have to perform from your heart. Your job is to entertain. When you entertain, your job is to allow the audience to relax, have fun, and leave wanting more. For me and many other entertainers, you become a different part of yourself because the stage elevates you higher than the audience. In a sense, it's like being a king in front of his kingdom. I have noticed that some entertainers live their day-to-day lives as though they are still on that stage and everyone around them has to look up to them to have a conversation. This is how this particular entertainer lives his life. As the years went on, his put-downs overshadowed his compliments, but for some strange reason I still put him up on a pedestal.

When I came home from California, I continued my weekend gig at a place called Zofia's. It was a Polish restaurant that became my home base for performing. I was there for two months at a time and I would leave my equipment there week after week. One evening as I approached my equipment table, I noticed a note sitting on top of my soundboard. My mouth dropped when I read the note. It said that I was a joke; I was not a singer; I was a comedian. My first reaction was one of anger. I knew exactly who had put the note there. For a moment, I just stood there, frozen and confused. How could anyone be so mean? Why would someone do this?

Then, all of a sudden, the confident person who had lived with the monks surfaced. Here's a person who wrote some pretty hurtful things. But then I stopped and thought: He took time out of his very busy day, sat down with a piece of paper and pen, and thought about me. Isn't that nice? Instead of taking time for himself doing something useful with his life, he wanted to put me down so he could feel better about himself. I forged ahead and had a great performance that night!

Here's how to **Overcome The Skateboard:**

You have to change your thoughts. How? First realize that you can't control what people will say or do. You can only control what you say or do. Don't allow people to consume your mind when it comes to negativity. Mahatma Gandhi said, "No one can hurt me without my permission." Don't give people permission. I don't hate this person whom I just talked about. If I say bad things about him, I am no different than him. Just because my actions are in defense to his invasion doesn't mean it's right. Even today, I occasionally go and see him perform. He has taught me to respect all performers for their own unique talents no matter what. Seeing him perform is a reminder for me that I can be in his presence and not get intimidated or nervous. He is just a man. I am just a man. We put our pants on one leg at a time.

If you ever want to worship someone, worship yourself for working towards making other people smile. Don't live from that pedestal because as a prophet once said, "Be humble for you are made of the earth. Be noble for you are made of the stars."

JUST BEING ME (A SONG I WROTE ABOUT THIS EXPERIENCE.)

WHEN I WAS JUST A LITTLE BOY
I LOVED TO SING AND DANCE
MOTHER'S DAY OF 1980
I GOT MY CHANCE.

BEFORE I TOOK THE STAGE THAT NIGHT
THE TEARS CAME TO MY EYES
BUT SOMETHING DEEP INSIDE OF ME
SAID GIVE IT A TRY.

SO I REACHED WAY DOWN
AND I BEGAN TO SEE
LIKE THE LION IN OZ
THE COURAGE HAS ALWAYS BEEN INSIDE OF ME.

BUT SOME PEOPLE BEGAN TO DOUBT ME
WHO DOES HE THINK HE IS?
THEY JOKED AND POKED FUN AT ME...
WHAT ARE YOU TRYING TO BE?

I'M NOT TRYING TO BE ANYTHING BUT ME.
I HAVE A DREAM BUT YOU DON'T KNOW WHAT I MEAN.
BUT YOU KEEP ON CRITICIZING YOU'LL GET NO SCENE FROM ME.
I'M NOT TRYING, I'M JUST BEING ME.

AS I GREW UP
MY CONFIDENCE DID TOO
BUT THE CRITICS WERE STILL THERE
SITTING IN THE CROWD
WHISPERING WITH A STARE.

SAY WHAT YOU WANT
YOUR THOUGHTS WON'T BRING ME DOWN.
THANK YOU FOR SPENDING YOUR TIME
THINKING ABOUT ME.
BUT DON'T YOU SEE THAT'S WHERE IT STARTS
A DREAM IS YOURS TO KEEP.
WHAT YOU DO WITH IT IS UP TO YOU.
NO ONE HAS THE RIGHT TO TAKE IT FROM YOU.

PEOPLE WILL BE CRITICAL
IT'S TYPICAL TO PUT YOU DOWN.
JUST SMILE AND CHUCKLE INSIDE.
BE YOURSELF AND NEVER NEVER HIDE.

I'M NOT TRYING TO BE ANYTHING BUT ME
I HAVE MY DREAM BUT YOU DON'T KNOW WHAT I MEAN.
BUT YOU KEEP ON CRITICIZING YOU'LL GET NO SCENE FROM ME
I'M NOT TRYING, I'M JUST BEING ME

©1999 Victor Pacini • www.victorpacini.com

30

THE DAY THE LIGHTS WENT OUT

"Death is a challenge. It tells us not to waste time...It tells us to tell each other right now that we love each other."
~Dr. Leo Buscaglia

As I write this chapter, I am sitting on a beautiful beach. The sun is reflecting on the water. It is a perfect place to write about someone I loved with all of my heart. Marianne Pacini was a quiet, shy woman who loved and was loved by her family, friends, and every person who crossed her path. This is not an exaggeration. Even though she was quiet, she was the glue that kept her family together. Let me rephrase that: She was the superglue that kept her family together despite all of the thunderstorms that attempted to break that bond. My father wore the pants in the family but my mother made sure he had those pants to wear. She was a great mom with an incredible heart. She lived for her kids and grandchildren.

In March of 1999, my parents left for what would be my mom's final vacation. My parents looked forward to trips to Las Vegas. It was a tradition, as well as a time for them to get away from the cold Chicago winters. I will never forget the phone call that came from my Uncle Jimmy. He told me my mom had suffered a heart attack at The Luxor Hotel. She passed away at the age of 59. I was devastated. My family was devastated. It was one of the most surreal moments of my life. After I received the phone call, I fell right into a friend's arms. My life changed forever.

My dad flew home from Las Vegas and told me that my mom sent me a card the day before her death. She always sent me cards. The day before her funeral, I checked my mailbox and sure enough, there it was. I opened the card and it said, "Even From Vegas I Miss You." I cried. To this day, I still look at it from time to time and imagine her fingerprints still on the card.

I call this chapter "The Day The Lights Went Out" because I felt like that when she died in Las Vegas, it was as if all of the lights went out on the Strip. Don't you think they should have closed all the casinos and cancelled the shows so they could pay respect to a woman who was loved by so many? It doesn't work that way. It's weird how life just keeps going on when people pass on. What I can say is that the lights temporarily went out for me the day my mom died.

Here's how to **Overcome The Skateboard:**

Understand, I have no regrets. I always told my mom I loved her at the end of every phone call. Even though the loss of my mom was painful and unbelievable, I was able to understand because I had no regrets. I had no choice but to accept her death. My heart still misses her very much. She wasn't here to see me get married or become a father. These thoughts are kind of hopeless because she is gone from my sight but she will never be gone from my heart and mind. That's where the focus must stay.

I know this may seem personal to ask, but is there anyone in your life that if they were to pass on, you would have regrets? If so, then start today and make the effort to spend more time with that person. Make that phone call and say hello. Do something that makes you feel good for that person. Regrets can be handled now while the person is still here rather than when it's too late. I have taken an inventory of people whom I love and done this regret exercise. It truly helps with this thing called death.

Another way I have dealt with my mom's death is I look for signs that tell me she is still with me. For example, my wife was due with our second baby on April 1st, 2008. On March 13th, she went into labor and Angelo was born on March 14th. My mom's birthday is March 14th. Think about it! Angelo could have been born on March 18th, 26th, 12th, or any other March day. He chose the 14th to make his grand entrance into this world. My mom was there to see that it happened that way. I believe it was her way of telling me, "Even from Heaven, I miss you, and I am with you on your journey of fatherhood."

> Love you Mom!
> Even from Vegas I miss you

A piece from the card she sent the day before her death • 1999

Victor and his mom • around 1981

VICTOR, IT'S TUCCI

"The most beautiful discovery true friends make is that they can grow separately without growing apart."
~Elizabeth Foley, spiritual teacher

A few months after my mom passed away, I wanted to go and stay at the hotel where she had the heart attack. This may seem strange, but I felt that she would communicate to me somehow. It was just a feeling inside of me. So my girlfriend Brenda and I jumped on a plane and went to Las Vegas.

Since my dad loved to gamble so much he was able to get us a very expensive room for next to nothing. When we saw the room I asked myself, "How much did he have to spend so we could stay here?" The Luxor Hotel is a very interesting hotel, shaped like a pyramid. We had a very beautiful room overlooking the pool.

I felt very connected with my mom because everywhere I looked I thought she might have been walking in that spot or playing on that slot machine. I felt very much at peace.

One day we were at the pool. It was another beautiful day in sunny Las Vegas. All of a sudden, I noticed a man playing with his kids in the pool. He looked like someone I knew but couldn't place. After a while, I happened to look at him again and it hit me. This guy was in the movie *Grease* with John Travolta. I knew it was him. I told Brenda who I thought it was and she said no way. I bet her $100 that it was him. I figured since we were in Las Vegas it was OK to bet. She took the bet and told me to go ask him. I told her that I didn't want to bother him because he was with his family and I thought that would be rude. I explained to her if it's meant to be, we will see him again and I will ask him then.

It's amazing how things happen. The next day Brenda and I were working out in the weight room at the hotel when in walked this mystery man. He proceeded to do some sit-ups. I was definitely in stalker mode because I couldn't get my eyes off of him. This was my big chance. I went up to him and said, "Hi, excuse me, are you an actor?" With a smile on his face he said, "Yes I am." I went on, "Were you in *Grease* with John Travolta?" He smiled again and said, "Yes I was. I played Sonny." "I knew it," I said. We began talking. His name is Michael Tucci and he could not have been any nicer to the two of us. He was playing in the musical *Chicago* at The Mandalay Bay Hotel and invited us to the show. What a great day it was in sunny Las Vegas. Not only did I meet a very humble movie actor but I won the bet. By the way, Brenda paid me.

Since I own my own business, I always make sure that wherever I go, I carry some of my marketing materials to pass out just in case. You never know who you are going to meet. I ended up giving Michael a copy of my song, "My Dreams", along with some information about my school programs. Not only did I have a great time with Brenda, I met someone who was kind enough to hear what I had to say about the music in my heart. Oh, by the way, not only did I leave Las Vegas feeling $100 richer, I had the chance to be where my mom was during her final days.

About three weeks later, I was home one night at my apartment in Glen Ellen, IL. I have to explain this apartment to you. This was my first apartment after living with my parents all of my life. It was a studio with one room and a kitchenette. The great thing about this is that you had to go through the closet to get to the bathroom. My closet was big enough to include my futon bed. It was a great set up. Every day I would wake up and look up and I could see what I wanted to wear that day. I was literally sleeping under my clothes rack.

I was lying in my bed watching TV and thinking about my mom. I was happy I went to Vegas but it had only been 6 months since her death. There was still a void. I guess it will always be there. All of a sudden the phone rang. I picked it up and the voice on the other end said, "Victor, it's Tucci, how are you?" He went on, "Victor, I have an idea. I want to make a TV show and I want you to play my son. We will call it *I'm The Father.*" (*The premise of the show is that Michael would play a teacher who was to retire at the end of the year. I come into his school and put on one of my assemblies for the kids. He sees me and realizes I am his son that he hasn't seen for almost twenty years. Ultimately, we get together and work together inspiring children to believe in themselves and follow their dreams.*)

I was stunned and excited at the same time. We talked for a while. When I got off the phone I began crying. This was such a surreal time for me. This was my mom talking to me. She brought Tucci into my life. I definitely believe that. Here's a guy who is the real deal when it comes to talent, and he is asking me to work with him. Up until then, I never really received that kind of response from people in the similar fields of music and performance. At the time, my friend Mark and I were working together on creating a multimedia type of educational show. He was so excited to hear this amazing news. We flew to Las Vegas to have a meeting with Michael.

All I can say is that the idea of making a show is incredible, but the work that goes into putting it together is unbelievable. For many months we worked diligently on this dream. Michael hired Juliet Johnson, a very talented up-and-coming writer, who put together an incredible treatment. I kept reminding myself to enjoy the process and not just think of the final goal. We had so much fun. Mark and I were like little kids in a candy store. Mark and I flew out to California a few times where we put on a live show at a school for some talent executives. I will never forget when I sang my song for the children and their families, and a couple came up to me afterward and told me they loved the song and I did a great job. After talking to them I knew who they were. It was Doug Savant and

Laura Leighton from the TV show called "Melrose Place." I think it's truly incredible that people who are excellent at what they do can compliment other people with respect and kindness.

After months and months of work, we finally had the chance to pitch this idea to Peter Engel, the executive producer of the hit show "Saved By The Bell". We sat in his office at NBC. This was a big deal! The presentation went very well and we were happy with our efforts.

They didn't buy the concept. We heard many reasons why they didn't think it would work. One was that it might have been too "goody goody" for television. Anyway, in our hearts and minds, it was still a great concept.

For almost a year and a half we worked together on something that had potential. Then all of sudden it was like the lights were turned off again. What went wrong? I kept asking myself, why didn't it work? Michael and I stopped talking as frequently. I think he put in so much of his energy and time, it came to a point for him to step back and focus on other things. Even though I was more upset of losing touch with him than losing the show, I respected his decision and continued living my dream.

A few years later, Juliet Johnson, the writer who worked on the pilot, called me. Ironically, I was in Vegas at the time. She thought the idea we had needed another chance. She believed in it so much. She gave it her all. We continue to pursue the dream but to no avail.

Here's how to **Overcome The Skateboard:**

Understand that everything happens for a reason. So what was the reason for all of this? It took a little time, but I believe it was just that phenomenal experience itself that I was supposed to have in my life. It opened many new doors for me. First of all, it gave me more confidence. Second, I had such an incredible time working with Michael, Juliet, and Mark. I wouldn't trade it for anything.

It also taught me about friendship. Elizabeth Foley's quote from the beginning of this chapter says it all. "The most beautiful discovery true friends make is that they can grow separately without growing apart." I became very close to Michael. Even though we didn't know each other very long, he became like a second dad to me. I have to be honest when I say that his abrupt departure from the project and our relationship affected me on a personal level. Right away, I thought what did I do? I have realized that it wasn't about me. In life, people do what they have to do given the circumstances of their lives. I was never angry. I overcame the skateboard by not taking things so personally. Our egos get in the way and we think everything is about us.

As far as the TV show not working out, I can live with that. In fact, I have lived without it. I got married four years ago to a beautiful woman. Yes, the same girl that lost the bet to me. I won more than $100 from her. I won her heart and now we have two beautiful children with a third on the way.

How did Michael overcome the skateboard? I can only give you my opinion, but I definitely think that he became a better person from this experience. He is now a theatre teacher in Southern California at an acclaimed College Preparatory High School. He is inspiring the youth of today by sharing his wisdom for life and knowledge of acting and theatre.

This quote about friendship really sums up the relationship I have with Michael Tucci. We reunited last year when he asked me to speak to his class. It was an incredible experience. I have and always will have the most utmost respect for Michael Tucci. Not only did he take time out of his life to work with me on something very special, but also he believed in me. I am up on that skateboard again and flying high.

Tucci and Victor at The Tucci Residence · 2003

Having fun for the camera · Victor, Tucci, & Mark · 2000

COURAGE

THE COURAGE OF A LION

"Close your eyes and tap your heels together three times. And think to yourself, there's no place like home."
~The Good Witch, The Wizard of Oz

Have you ever seen "The Wizard of Oz?" Growing up, it was one of my favorite movies. I loved the characters and the idea of a yellow brick road. The lion was a character that looked for and tried to obtain courage. He thought it was located outside of himself. Many of us search for happiness, contentment, inner peace, and love by going outside of ourselves. We think that if we can't find it, it doesn't exist. If we only stopped and took a look at ourselves. As for courage, I don't know anyone with more than my sister Reneé. First of all, she loved the lion and was able to imitate him perfectly. She made us laugh time and time again.

She displayed an insurmountable amount of courage on September 3, 2001. On that day I received a phone call from a police officer who informed me that my sister and brother-in-law were involved in a shooting. They were both airlifted to different hospitals.

When my family and I arrived at the hospital we found out that Reneé had been shot four times by her husband. He then shot himself. My sister was in surgery for many hours to repair the damage the bullet caused when it hit her abdomen. I will never forget when we saw her that evening. She opened her eyes and said she had an itch on her nose. We removed the oxygen and scratched it for her. She then closed her eyes. Three weeks later my beautiful sister with the courage of a lion passed away. She was 39 years old. I was devastated, as was my family. You read about these events in newspapers and see them on the television but they never happen to you. All I can say is I was pushed off my skateboard. At that moment I couldn't see how I would get up. It seemed impossible.

That first night I decided, with the help of Brenda, to go visit my brother-in-law in the hospital. When I entered the room I saw the same pain. His family cried, too. They suffered, too. For me, I wanted to see him because I couldn't understand why he would do something like that. He was still my brother-in-law. I looked at him and cried. He died the next day.

For those three weeks while my sister lay in bed, I cried more and more. I was sad and kept asking why? It didn't take long until I realized that asking why was truly a dead-end street. There's no answer to it. There is only our speculation to reasons behind the madness. I switched my question from "why" to "what can I do with this?" I decided to think about ways in which I could make a difference for my nieces who are alive and in need of love and attention. In the matter of a month they were without parents. That made me extremely sad but it inspired me to do something. It also made me realize how grateful I was to have had my mom in my life for 27 years. Here I am feeling sorry for myself because my mom didn't see me get married or have children, and my nieces will never have the opportunity to talk to their parents or go on vacation, or even get a much-needed hug.

I had to act quickly. I wanted to do something for them. They were going to be raised by my oldest sister Michele. Here is another sister with courage. I am so grateful that Michele and her husband Rich took these girls into their home. They have three children of their own and now the dynamic has changed. It was a transition for Michele's kids as well. (It's amazing to me how many people get affected by one person's selfish act.) For me, I decided to take action with what I know best. I love to perform. I thought I could put on a benefit and all the money raised would go into a college account for my nieces. As the years passed, I created The Neysaké Foundation. My nickname for my sister was Ney Ney, so it's a foundation for Reneé's sake, hence Neysaké.

I never go a day without thinking about Reneé, a woman who made me laugh so much. She was loved by everyone. She was the type of person who would help others before herself. She is now and forever my Ney Ney.

Here's how to **Overcome The Skateboard:**

I was able to get back on the board as soon as I changed my thoughts. Once I changed the question from why to what I could do, the answers starting coming to me. I believe it's easy to go into a bedroom, pull the shades down and covers over your head, and feel sorry about the circumstances of your life. It's more of a challenge to take responsibility for the way you respond to circumstances and take action that will ultimately make a difference.

I will never forget visiting my brother-in-law in the hospital the evening of this unforgettable event. I saw him and I cried. I saw his family and I cried. They were all sleeping on the floor, praying for him. They fell off their skateboards, too. I realized in my heart this was not two sides of a war. I wasn't visiting the enemy. I was visiting a family who was crying the same tears as our family. In essence, I was visiting my family. After all, we are all one on this planet.

I don't think a lot about my brother-in-law these days. If I do, I reflect on the fun we had as a family. Gandhi said, "Hate the sin, love the sinner." As difficult as it may seem I decided to adopt that phrase. For me, it's allowed me to focus on "A Night For Reneé" and ask, How may I serve?

MY THOUGHTS ARE THE OBSTACLE

"Do you want to meet the love of your life? Look in the mirror."
~Byron Katie

Byron Katie is a woman who I have so much respect for. She is an author, speaker, and the creator of <u>The Work</u>, a process that consists of four questions and a turnaround. The purpose is to question our stressful thoughts and ultimately the thought lets go of you. She says, "It's not our thoughts, but the attachment to our thoughts, that cause suffering." She continues: "There are three kinds of business in the world: mine, yours, and God's. If you are living your life and I am mentally living your life, who is here living mine? We're both over there. Being mentally in your business keeps me from being present in my own. I am separate from myself, wondering why my life doesn't work."

All of this takes place in our minds. Have you ever been upset? I am sure you have. Can you remember who you were thinking about at the time of being upset?

Whose business were you in? Ultimately, you owe yourself to stay in your business and cultivate your garden and not worry about the other gardens that you see.

Once again, I can't stress enough that life happens. With life comes situations that occur beyond your control. My growth as a person has come from an ability to see all obstacles as opportunities for growth. These opportunities are always present but we choose not to see them. You have to practice at changing your "why does this always happen to me" kind of thinking. Negative thoughts are just thoughts.

What I am working on right now in my life are self-defeating thoughts. Have you ever beaten yourself up mentally? I know that I have and still do sometimes. For example, I speak for a living. I talk to people of all ages about believing in yourself. Sometimes, I don't think I am capable. Who am I to stand in front of an audience and share this wisdom with people? Then I sit back and understand that this is my passion and my calling and I am a work-in-progress. I am also very good at what I do. And then a question comes up in my mind: If I am very good at this, why do I have these self-defeating thoughts?

You have to learn to not take yourself so seriously. I have a suggestion for you right now. Put down this book and go right into the bathroom and look into the mirror. When you see your reflection looking back at you, make a funny face at yourself. This will cause you to smile. Understand that when you look at yourself the only one looking back at you, is you! It's not your dad, mom, brother, sister, not even your dog. Now look at yourself and say, "Hey, I love you." Start practicing today the act of keeping thoughts that strengthen you and ridding yourself of ones that weaken you.

A drawing a student gave Victor for his book, "My Dreams".

CHOOSE KINDNESS

"You cannot do a kindness too soon, for you never know how soon it will be too late."
~Ralph Waldo Emerson

Winning within is about how you can improve yourself during the difficult times in your life, but it goes further than that. You become a winner within when you go out and give of yourself. I am a firm believer that there is nothing better than putting a smile on someone's face. Smiles are contagious and magical. Have you ever walked around at school or work and felt terribly sick? Someone comes up to you, smiles, and says, "hi." Don't you forget that you are sick for a few moments? Of course you do! Smiles are one way of giving but there are many other ways that can make a difference.

I was in the drive thru lane at Starbucks, ordered my coffee, and proceeded to pull up and pay. As I pulled to the window the cashier said that the person in front of me paid for my coffee. I drove away trying to catch up to the person but they were gone before I could say thank you.

That's an unusual act of kindness but one I will never forget. Who does this? That person paid for my coffee and I bet she had a great day. I drove away amazed!

Another time I was stopped at a red light when a motorcycle turned the corner and lost control and fell right in the middle of the street. I automatically put my car in park and went to the victim's aid. I asked him how badly he was hurt. He was pinned under the motorcycle. I immediately picked up the bike and helped him to the sidewalk. Someone called 9-1-1 and he was on his way to recovery. Now, this act was something I think anyone would do. The point here is it gave me a good feeling inside as I drove away. That's the power of acts of kindness. They make both parties feel good.

Kindness is another choice you must make to feel good. I can guarantee that the more acts of kindness you do for yourself and others the more you will create positive chemical reactions inside of you. The Random Acts Of Kindness Foundation says, "Stress-related health problems improve after performing kind acts. Helping reverses feelings of depression, supplies social contact, and decreases feelings of hostility and isolation that can cause stress, overeating, ulcers, etc. A drop in stress may, for some people, decrease the constriction within the lungs that leads to asthma attacks."

I used to work for Starlight Foundation. One component of the organization is as follows: "Starlight brings together experts from pediatric health care, technology and entertainment to create programs that educate, entertain and inspire seriously ill children." Once a month, I would go to a children's nursing home in downtown Chicago and entertain the children. These children would dance in their wheel chairs. I will never forget one boy who was hooked up to IV's and could barely move. Once I started singing he smiled from ear to ear. What I learned from all of this is that we can never dismiss people. Everyone has something to teach us.

Author Joann C. Jones wrote, "During my second year of nursing school our professor gave us a quiz. I breezed through the questions until I read the last one: "What is the first name of the woman who cleans the school?" Surely this was a joke. I had seen the cleaning woman several times, but how would I know her name? I handed in my paper, leaving the last question blank. Before the class ended, one student asked if the last question would count toward our grade. "Absolutely," the professor said. "In your careers, you will meet many people. All are significant. They deserve your attention and care, even if all you do is smile and say hello." I've never forgotten that lesson. I also learned her name was Dorothy."

Being kind and showing that you care can create incredible experiences not only for the intended receiver but also to the person who is performing the kind act.

Here's how to **Overcome The Skateboard:**

Choose to do an act of kindness for someone else. It will take your mind off any obstacle and you will make a difference. It might also calm you down, and you will be able to see the obstacle in a different light.

Here's a challenge: Do something for the person who you have a conflict with. Someone once said that it's easy to do something nice for people who smell good, but it's more of a challenge to do something nice for people who just plain smell!

When I had that experience with the person who left that negative note on my equipment, I sent him a copy of my book, My Dreams. It made me feel really good because I became a stronger person. I took Byron Katie's teachings and decided to stay in my business and do what made me feel good.

I end this chapter with a favorite story that I use in my talks. It's by Anonymous whom I would love to meet some day. The story is called, "The Circus."

"Once when I was a teenager, my father and I were standing in line to buy tickets for the circus. Finally, there was only one family between us and the ticket counter.

"This family made a big impression on me. There were eight children, all probably under the age of 12. You could tell they didn't have a lot of money. Their clothes were not expensive, but they were clean.

"The children were well-behaved, all of them standing in line, two-by-two behind their parents, holding hands. They were excitedly jabbering about the clowns, elephants and other acts they would see that night. One could sense they had never been to the circus before. It promised to be a highlight of their young lives.

"The father and mother were at the head of the pack standing proud as could be. The mother was holding her husband's hand, looking up at him as if to say, "You're my knight in shining armor." He was smiling and basking in pride, looking at her as if to reply, "You got that right."

"The ticket lady asked the father how many tickets he wanted. He proudly responded, "Please let me buy eight children's tickets and two adult tickets so I can take my family to the circus."

"The ticket lady quoted the price. The man's wife let go of his hand, her head dropped, the man's lip began to quiver. The father leaned a little closer and asked, "How much did you say?"

"The ticket lady again quoted the price. The man didn't have enough money.

"How was he supposed to turn and tell his eight kids that he didn't have enough money to take them to the circus?

"Seeing what was going on, my dad put his hand into his pocket, pulled out a $20 bill and dropped it on the ground. (We were not wealthy in any sense of the word.) My father reached down, picked up the bill, tapped the man on the shoulder and said, "Excuse me, sir, this fell out of your pocket."

"The man knew what was going on. He wasn't begging for a handout but certainly appreciated the help in a desperate, heartbreaking, embarrassing situation. He looked straight into my dad's eyes, took my dad's hand in both of his, squeezed tightly onto the $20 bill, and with his lip quivering and a tear streaming down his cheek, he replied, 'Thank you, thank you, sir. This really means a lot to me and my family.'

"My father and I went back to our car and drove home. We didn't go to the circus that night, but we didn't go without."

TRUE NOBILITY

"When you are content to be simply yourself and don't compare or compete, everybody will respect you."
~Lao Tzu

We have been taught in our society that competing against others is the norm. The goal is to win a trophy, an award, personal praises, etc. I am not against competing; however, what I am talking about is a way to live a more enlightened life. It's called True Nobility. Wayne Dyer said that, "True Nobility is not about being better than anyone else, it's about being better than you used to be." I think that simplifies it. You don't have to be better than anyone else. Who has the better G.P.A.? How much does he make? When it comes to these kinds of superficial possessions, you will sometimes win and sometimes lose. What I am talking about is winning all of the time. What have you done today that makes you a better person than yesterday? If there is one concept I would love for you to truly digest it is this concept called True Nobility. If winning trophies is a passion of yours, my suggestion is to not get possessed by them. I have trophies from little league baseball, but they don't define me. It was simply my reward for dedicating myself to being a good baseball player. Now that I look back, the real reward was becoming a better ball player and working successfully with a team.

What makes you happy? I'm not talking outside of you. You have it inside. Take one positive quality about yourself and let it surround you for the day. Remind yourself throughout the day about that quality. Let it soak into your heart and mind for 24 hours. Then each day ask yourself, "How am I a little bit better today than I was yesterday"?

This book is ultimately about you. Love has to start with you or it doesn't start at all. Before you can respect anyone, you have to respect yourself first. Once you have this quality for yourself then you can give it away. Dr. Leo Buscaglia said, "Love yourself—accept yourself—forgive yourself—and be good to yourself, because without you the rest of us are without a source of many wonderful things."

Everything I have said here is really about taking action. Teachers will put their heart and soul out there for you but it's up to you to learn and understand. Parents will be there for you but it's up to you to communicate your feelings with respect and dignity. Dan Millman, the author of The Laws of Spirit said this about action. "Turning ideas into action requires energy, sacrifice, courage, and heart, because to act is to risk. We have to overcome all the good reasons to put it off, to let someone else do it, to remain in the easy chair of good intentions. It's better to do what is best than not do it and have a good excuse."

Be willing to fall off your skateboard and know that getting up is up to you. If you choose to get up and keep riding, know that other bumps in the road are likely but how you respond to those bumps will be up to you as well. When you respond from a peaceful place, the quality of your life will propel you to new levels. You will be better than you used to be. Now, that's a TRUE VICTORY!

Victor's original prints

Victor's original prints

NOT BEHIND A COMPUTER

"And in the end, it's not the years in your life that count. It's the life in your years."
~Abraham Lincoln

I love to sing but I realized that an education was also something I really wanted to pursue. After receiving help for my abuse, I decided to take off a semester of school so I could work and think about what I really wanted to be when I grow up. I was a little stressed out after graduating high school because I didn't exactly know what I wanted to do with my life.

It's amazing to me that high school students are supposed to know what they want to do with their lives by the time they leave school. I remember in high school it was always about going to college and getting a job. Please understand, jobs are important but the above quote by Abraham Lincoln is really the foundation for getting a job that makes you want to feel good. If we could just teach that to children when they are younger, then by the time they get to high school they may be more understanding of what they are passionate about in life.

I decided to attend a community college so I could begin my journey to a bachelor's degree. As I was sitting at Harper College one day after taking my placement tests, my name was called. I thought I did something wrong. It's amazing how our brain automatically thinks something negative. Who knew that all of the difficult times I had up until that moment would lead to something magnificent? I found out that because I graduated in the top 5% of my high school class, I was eligible for a full scholarship. I finally felt that my hard work in high school paid off.

I decided to take all of my required courses along with some art classes. As I dove into advanced drawing, figure drawing, and graphics, I soon realized that there was a field called graphic design. I became excited. I was a great student with an inner drive to do well. For the next two years I majored in Art and continued to take my other classes, too. I also got a job as the computer graphics aide. I loved it. I helped other students and little did I know it was really the beginning of my calling.

After I graduated from Harper College, I transferred to Columbia College in Chicago where I majored in graphic design. I really loved this because I was able to create art pieces that really came from my heart. I designed from a perspective of personal healing. Because each piece came from the heart, my grades reflected that dedication. Obviously I couldn't do that with every class but I loved it nonetheless. I graduated with honors with a B.A. degree in Graphic Design in 1995. I was so excited that I knew it wouldn't take long to find a job.

I started working for a company a few months after college. This company was located in a house and my office was in the basement. This job was interesting for two reasons. First, the owners of the company were husband and wife and they were just starting up a brand new design company. They wanted a designer so they could go out and do the selling. It made sense to me. They were very friendly people. The second reason why it was so interesting was the fact that their business was out of their basement.

I was so excited when they offered me the job. I enjoyed it for a few weeks. Then, all of a sudden, I began feeling bored and unfulfilled. I expressed my feelings with my parents and they told me to be a little patient. Something didn't feel right. Maybe it was the environment, maybe it was the type of designing I was doing, or maybe it was the fact I was alone in a basement. I decided after a few months to look for another job. I have been told you are supposed to give a job at least a year before you make a decision like this one. I guess the reasoning is if it's less than a year it's not resumé friendly. Anyway, I didn't listen to most people and I found another job in the graphic design field.

This environment was totally different. It was an actual building and I had a real office. This was going to be better. I was going to be happy. This was my dream job.

After a few months, I began having those same feelings of unhappiness that I had at my previous job. I kept thinking to myself, "Am I going to sit behind a computer for the rest of my life?" I realized that I love to design and I love to create. I just don't necessarily want to work for other people. Actually, I do want to create for others but if it comes from me and I do it on my own terms. You have to listen to your burning desire inside of your heart.

I was at a career fair once for high school students who are going on to college. Students that wanted to become singers and authors came up to me. They asked a lot of questions. I had answers for most of them. When I was asked, "What if it doesn't work out?" I answered, "Then at least you gave it a shot. Who knows? You never know unless you try." Dr. Wayne Dyer said, "Love what you do and do what you love."

Here's how to **Overcome The Skateboard:**

The obstacle here was what was I going to do with my life when I seemed so confused and frustrated. If you are at the same point right now in your life I would say it's OK. This is where you are, and for me, I am a firm believer that where you are is perfect and it will lead you to the next place. All of these so-called obstacles with my jobs were all stepping-stones to building my own business.

Napoleon Hill, in a book titled <u>Think and Grow Rich</u> said, "If the thing you wish to do is right, and you believe in it, go ahead and do it! Put your dream across and never mind what "they" say if you meet with temporary defeat, for "they," perhaps, do not know that every failure brings with it the seed of an equivalent success."

MR. P, CAN I SING WITH YOU?

"Don't die with your music still in you."
~Dr. Wayne Dyer

Dr. Dyer said, "Don't die with your music still in you." To me, it's probably one of the most important quotes I have ever read and committed to memory.

I lost the passion I had in college. I lost my excitement. What was wrong with me? I left the graphic design field for the time being. I had to do something. My girlfriend's mother recommended me for a job at an elementary school. I would be an aide in the music department, art department, and P.E. department. It was right down my alley. It reminded me of the time I was the aide in the graphics department at Harper College. I took it with a smile and with a newfound excitement.

These kids were great. I felt like a kid again. Part of my duty was to be outside with them during recess. I had to make sure no one was getting into trouble. I felt so much like a kid that I played football with the kids almost every day. It was a blast.

Then one day, I asked the principal if I could perform for the students. I wanted to show them what Mr. P does in the nightclubs on the weekends. He thought it was a great idea. I will never forget what happened next.

I was outside one day when a 6th. grader named Matt came up to me. "Mr. P, I heard you are going to sing for us." "That's right." I said. "Can I sing with you?" asked Matt with a smile. I said, "Sure, that would be great." Little did I know that this was the beginning of something amazing. Matt has Down's Syndrome and I thought this would help his confidence. We practiced a song called "Johnny B. Goode" by Chuck Berry.

The day of the show, I called Matt up to the stage. With no sign of fear, he belted out the tune with me. The students gave him a standing ovation. He then put his hands up in the air as if he had won a gold medal!

After the show, a teacher came up to me and told me that I had something special with kids. She told me that there are people that travel all around and put on shows for kids. I thought that was very cool, but I had no idea where to start, so I kept searching for my calling.

After doing some thinking, I decided I wanted to be a teacher. After all, that teacher told me I was good with children so it sounded like a perfect fit. I found out that there was a Master's program available to people who had a B.A. in something else than education. You teach during the day, go to school at night, and they actually pay you for your teaching services. I applied and was accepted.

The summer of 1996 I entered DePaul University with the intention of obtaining a Masters Degree in education. There was only one problem. I couldn't forget what that teacher asked me back at the elementary school. Could I sing songs and inspire children? I didn't know what that meant.

That summer I purchased a white Mazda Miata from my uncle. I loved it. I am really not into cars but I just loved having a convertible. My friend's grandfather called it "the chick magnet." As I was driving downtown to school for my first day, I had an epiphany. I knew what I truly wanted to do with my life. I wanted to start my own company and design empowering programs and products for children. I marched right up to my advisor and told her my dream. Let's just say she wasn't too happy about my dream. Who could blame her? They invested time, money, and energy for me to be part of this program. Let's not forget all of the people that recommended me for acceptance. Ultimately, you have to listen to your heart. That's exactly what I did.

I left DePaul University with the most freeing feeling I had ever experienced. I had a purpose. I had a burning desire inside and it wanted to come out and be shared with the world.

I had to share it with my parents first. My mom was disappointed and upset with me. My dad supported me from the beginning. After I talked with my mom, she soon realized this was my life and she would support whatever choices I made.

Sometimes, we don't know what's in store for us. I never thought I would go to schools and inspire children. I had been a professional singer since the age of eight, so who knew that I could combine the spoken word with songs? Let's not forget I graduated with a degree in Graphic Design. I needed someone to design my marketing materials, business cards, etc. It was all falling into place perfectly. I have to say that's how my life has been. Things always seems to work out in some way.

Here's how to **Overcome The Skateboard:**

I want to close this chapter out with something I call "The Lucky Penny Analogy". I need you to use your imagination for a second here. Go back to a time when you were nine years old. Let's say you are walking down the street and you stumble upon a penny. You reach down, pick it up and squeeze it real tight. Let's also say that the penny is your personal dream. You might want to be a doctor, a singer, a teacher, or whatever. You take that penny and run home and tell your family about your dream. Your family loves you so much that hopefully they will support your dream. One day, however, someone comes up to you and says, "You want to be a doctor, you're not smart enough, or you want to sing, you're a joke, you can't." So you take this penny and your dream and you put it in your pocket and in the back of your mind, and it stays there for the rest of your life. You have just allowed someone to keep you from attempting your dream.

There will be people out there who will try to keep you down with their negative comments. They will succeed only if you allow them to succeed. Don't forget what the great Buddha said, "When someone offers you a gift and you refuse to accept that gift, to whom does the gift belong?" When someone offers you his or her negative criticism, don't accept it. One more thing: Don't squeeze that penny so tightly in your hand. When you squeeze anything too tight nothing new can get in. By holding it gently in your hand it allows for old dreams to leave and new ones to manifest. Finally, take the gift that Wayne Dyer gave to me: "Don't die with your music still in you."

Victor's original prints

I AM READY TO GO ON TOUR NOW

"I want to know if you can live with failure yours and mine and still stand at the edge of the lake and shout to the silver of the full moon, "yes"..."
~Oriah Mountain Dreamer

My friend Bill Selep once told me if someone wants to pay me to perform I should always say yes. Even if I thought I deserved more, he said I should still do it. I will never forget when he said: "Junior, you never know who will be sitting in the audience." He was definitely very savvy when it came to business. Over the years I have kept an open mind because of my friend and I have adopted a very important belief. Whatever it is that you want to accomplish, don't have the mindset that you feel you are entitled to it. There are a million people that want to do what you want to do, and it will never happen if you just sit on your behind and wait for people to come knocking on your door. That's just the way it is. You can have all of the talent, all of confidence, all of the chutzpah, but if you don't have the willingness to get yourself out there, the door will stay closed.

In 1997, I opened a door for myself and it changed my life forever. In fact, I went knocking on someone else's door. By now, you know I am an Elvis fan. In 1979, a man by the name of Ronnie McDowell came onto the music scene with a song he wrote called, "The King is Gone". He became an overnight success because he sounded so much like Elvis. As time went on he wanted his own identity. He became a very popular country singer and had many hits in the 1980's. He was hired multiple times to be the voice of Elvis in a few made-for-TV movies about the life of The King.

This is where my brother inspired me once again. He collected Ronnie McDowell's music over the years and turned me on to it as well. In my mind, I had a list of dreams that I wanted to accomplish one day. One of them was to perform with Ronnie McDowell.

I had a crazy idea. Victor Hugo said, "There's nothing more powerful than an idea whose time has come." This was an idea and it was time to try it. I would put on a concert and I would hire Ronnie to be the main act. I would be his opening act. Why not?

I did it! On May 4, 1997 one of my dreams came true. It was an incredible experience because not only did I open my own door for myself, I also sang with this incredible performer. I had a plan, though. I really thought that he would ask me to come on the road and be his opening act. I just thought that would be the natural progression of this once-in-a lifetime experience. I was wrong. Out of respect to Ronnie, he came, did his job, and moved on to the next gig. I had planned for months for this concert. I wanted to wow him and impress him. It was over in four hours. I was so high and then boom, I crashed emotionally. I was really thinking that this was the beginning of the next step in my singing career. I actually think I might have gone into a mild depression. I went right back to performing at the little nightclubs. It was a very strange time for me. Not even the enlightened person who went to the Buddhist Monastery could be found at this time.

Here's how to **Overcome The Skateboard:**

It didn't take long for me to get out of my funk. The reality was he didn't want to take me on tour with him. I had two choices: Feel sorry for myself and blame it on him, or take responsibility and learn from it. By now, you know what I did. It's simple. I decided to learn from this experience. Number 1: Here's an opportunity to focus on what went right and what I could learn from this master. Number 2: Don't put all of eggs in one basket or you might end up with scrambled emotions.

I just learned to be more interactive with my audience. Ronnie McDowell makes his audiences feel important by talking to them. He gets them involved by letting them sing with him. He controls his audience so when he needs to do something that requires them to watch and listen, he is effortless and it comes off seamless. He is a true entertainer.

For many months, I poured my heart and soul into a project. I think that is definitely commendable. The problem with that is I went in with the attitude that I was entitled to earn the role of opening act. I figured he would see me perform and just open the door to his super duper tour bus and say "hop in." I had high hopes. It's great to have high hopes so long as you are not attached to them. Remember what I said about the Lucky Penny. Don't squeeze it too tightly. When you bank on one idea, you are blinded to other potential new ideas and concepts. I never got a chance to tour with Ronnie McDowell. However, if I had, I might not be writing my own songs and being a visionary entertainer by inspiring young and old to believe in themselves.

Victor & Ronnie in Wisconsin Dells. · 1997

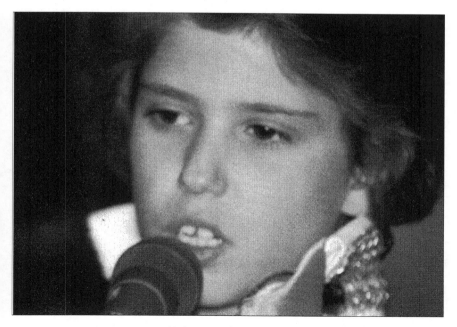

Victor on stage · 1982

Victor & Ronnie sharing the stage · 1997

Victor sharing the stage with his daughter · 2007

A NIGHT FOR RENEÉ

"The desire of gold is not for gold. It is for the means of freedom and benefit."
~Ralph Waldo Emerson

After a few years of putting on a benefit to raise money for my two nieces, my sister Michele pulled me aside one day. She told me that the kids would be fine from a financial standpoint and that she didn't feel comfortable taking money from people every year. She respectfully asked me to stop the yearly benefits for the children. It only took me a short time to redirect my focus. I knew in my heart I could not stop. After all, this gathering had turned into not only a good cause but also a therapy session for the parties involved. In a sense, I was being selfish, but I think for a good reason.

This event has literally become a Night For Reneé-- a night to remember an amazingly courageous woman and at the same time, a night to honor women who are currently going through what Reneé went through, but are alive to receive the support.

I will never forget my sister or any of the negative memories that caused her death. But I can focus more in-depth on the happy times I shared with her and the joy she brought to me. I can also focus on the good that has come from this tragedy. Make no mistake about it, this was a tragedy beyond anything I could have imagined, but I chose to live my life from a place of forgiveness, peace, and what I could do for Reneé now that she is not here to do things herself.

Reneé was a woman who helped. I know without any doubts in my mind she would have been there for other women who needed help. I decided to continue this benefit and focus on raising awareness and money for women in need. For the last few years I have been working closely with WINGS (Women In Need Growing Stronger).

This event has grown into a magical evening of love. What amazes me is the support from family, friends, and people I have met because of this event who have stepped up in ways that I never thought were possible. My co-chair for the event has been in my life since I was just a child. She has a special connection to this event not only because of me, but also the love she shared for Reneé. She has been the glue for this event. She may argue otherwise, but I know the truth.

I will not forget that my brothers and sisters and my father fell off their skateboard in this situation. We fell off together. I cannot and will not try to answer how they have coped with Reneé's death. Everyone has his or her own way. I can say how proud I am of this group and their ability to become a closer family because of it. My siblings are the most forgiving people I know. Each one of them has been transformed in some way.

I have never forced anyone in my family to be part of the benefit. This benefit is my way of handling the pain. My brother and sisters have their own personal ways of dealing with this situation. There is no right or wrong. There is only what's right for each individual. I love them so much! They attend the benefit every year and help bring more people for support. I will say that my sister Laura has stepped up in a big way this year. Laura had her share of overcoming the skateboards in her life. She has participated on the committee and has done a great job. I think she feels more connected to Reneé by being involved in the evening. I think it's a way of healing for her.

This journey we call life is a roller coaster of events. Despite the difficulties at times, I know it's worth riding.

From left to right (Top):
Victor, Laura, Reneé, Michele, Angelo, Larry & Marianne

THE PUNCH THAT SAVED MY LIFE

"An eye for eye only ends up making the whole world blind."
Gandhi

I have always been attracted to the philosophy of Gandhi. Here was a man who stood up for millions of people but he did it without violence. To me, he was an underdog because he was up against people who were quite a bit stronger and with many more resources. Still, he didn't give up. He moved forward and kept getting up on his skateboard. If I knew of his philosophy when I was younger, then the story I am about to share with you could have been avoided. However, I wouldn't have changed it for anything because I am who I am due to the outcome of this event.

By now, you have a general idea of how my childhood affected my life. I have to say that the problems at home and my abuse may have contributed to this confrontation. I don't know, but boy, did I learn a lesson. As I recall, I was a good kid but occasionally thought I was better than other boys. All I can say is that this incident happened for a reason and I am so glad it turned out the way it did.

It was a spring night at the Lions Park Elementary School Fun Fair. I was a fifth grader with a small attitude. I went with a group of friends. We entered the fun fair like a bunch of 21 year olds entering a bar looking for a fight. I always had a conflict with this boy named Chris. Well, this was the night for fun at the Fun Fair. I will never forget how it started. We were verbally yelling at each other and decided to take it outside. A group of kids surrounded us in a circle. There I was on-stage again. This time I wasn't singing "Love Me Tender." Before I could get my arms up in the air, I saw a clenched fist hit me right smack dab in the face. All I can remember is falling to the ground. I began crying. It didn't seem like anyone wanted to help me. That was it! The boy who was so cool froze in his tracks.

I would be lying to you if I said I wasn't humiliated and embarrassed by what happened. Since everyone was standing around me, I couldn't run away and pretend like it didn't happen. My friends looked at me differently; however, they still liked me. Even Chris looked at me differently because from that moment on I became someone he picked on during my elementary days and the junior high days. I will never forget all the times he tried to fight me on the playground in junior high. I never tried to start anything with him. I don't know if it was out of fear or maybe, just maybe, I had grown. I think it was a little bit of both.

Here's how to **Overcome The Skateboard:**

I think getting punched was the best thing that ever happened to me. Now that I look back it really and truly made me who I am today. Let's just say that I would have won that fight. I would have walked away with more confidence for fighting. I would have gone on to junior high and picked on kids like me. I would have gained all of this momentum towards negative behavior. That's what Chris did when he won the fight. There may have been other circumstances in his life that I don't know about. All I know is that what we do now paints a picture for what happens later. That doesn't mean you can't change your life at any given time. What you do today has the potential of molding certain future behaviors.

I remember how my life changed. I went from being a little bully to a very helpful, respectful, and kind young boy. I will never forget I was in English class when I went to my teacher to ask a question. She was in the middle of a conversation at the time. I said, "Excuse me but I have a question." I will never forget that she commended me on being so polite. Little things like that began showing up in my life. When I went on to junior high I was approached by my art teacher who showed an interest in my work. He worked with me and helped me with my projects. Once again, if I would have won that fight, it is very possible that I would have gone on to junior high showing no interest in art whatsoever. Everything happens for a reason.

I forgot about the punch that saved my life in high school because by then I was really focused on my schoolwork and baseball. I remember having a class with Chris during my senior year. It seemed like a lifetime ago since the fight but we talked as if nothing ever happened. He went down his path and I went down mine. He was a confident fighter and I was a confident student who graduated in the top 5% in my class. I don't say this to brag, but to let you know that anything is possible. I do believe that punch caused a chain of events that led me to all of my accomplishments after The Fun Fair at Lions Park Elementary School.

IMPOSSIBLE

"The impossible — what nobody can do until somebody does."
~Unknown

I love the quote at the top. Haven't you ever thought it's impossible or I can't? I think that's been in our minds a few times. I have always been compelled to follow my gut on ways to propel my career in high gear. Like the Ronnie McDowell experience, I have learned to not be so attached to situations. You do what you want and then let go of the outcome. One person who has taught me so much about letting go is Dr. Wayne Dyer. I have quoted him many times in this book. In life, you have to learn from people who inspire you. Whatever it is that you want to do, you find someone who is doing it already and ask them many empowering questions. It's called being like-minded. Right around the time of The Ronnie McDowell Concert, I began listening and reading anything that I felt could help me get to that next level in my life. I dove into the work of Dr. Wayne Dyer because his work is truly inspirational and practical.

I began to remember the philosophy that people will not bang down my door. If I want anything it is me that must get up and take action. I began writing letters to great authors, media people, and anyone that might be interested in my message. What is really cool about Dr. Wayne Dyer is that he made it a point to write you back with a signed book. Once I sent him a copy of my book, <u>My Dreams</u>. I thought maybe he would be inspired. You never know who ultimately will get their hands on your material.

A friend of mine told me Dr. Dyer would be speaking at a local high school. It was sponsored by the local hospital. This was not the typical venue for him and it was limited seating. I set out to see him. I sat in the front row and just soaked in everything he was talking about. I kept thinking that after he finished, he was probably going to be busy out in front signing autographs and taking pictures with people. I had to act fast. After the program, I followed him back stage. He met me and I walked with him to the front. While we were walking I asked him if he ever received the book I sent him. He said he really liked it and gave it to his granddaughter. I thought that was cool. I took it a step further. I then asked him if I could sing a song for his audience someday. You never know unless you ask. He told me that if he had known I was in the audience he would have invited me to sing. That was my chance and I lost it.

I didn't give up. He came back to Chicago a few months later for his "Power of Intention Tour". This time there were a few thousand people in the audience. My friend Mark came along with me. I also brought a copy of my song to sing just in case.

During the intermission I went up to Wayne and said hello. He didn't hesitate. He asked me if I wanted to sing. I was speechless but acted very cool and said yes. My friend who happened to work with an audio-visual company in Chicago ran up and told the tech to start the CD when it was time.

This is the best part. When he introduced me he called me "the pain in the ass from Chicago". He said it in a fun way. I got up there and did a great job. It actually led to a future speaking engagement.

When you think something is impossible you act as though it's impossible and you never can find the opportunities that could help you. When I was 27 years old I wrote down the word IMPOSSIBLE and just looked at it. I realized that if you look at it differently the word changes.

IMPOSSIBLE
Now change the way you look at it.

I'M POSSIBLE
The same letters, just spaced differently.

Here's how to **Overcome The Skateboard:**

I overcame this skateboard by not giving up. I knew that I was acting from a very genuine place so going backstage was a risk worth taking. There was something inside me that told me to talk to Dr. Dyer. He would not come to me.

All of these experiences would probably not have happened in my life if I had not taken the initial action to get them started. My business was just an idea. I wasn't aware of the possibilities until that teacher approached me. That teacher would not have approached me if I hadn't taken the job at the school. It's about taking action and understanding that falling off the skateboard is OK. If it doesn't work out, so what? You have to be willing to try.

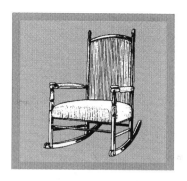

THE ROCKING CHAIR

"Don't wait. The time will never be just right."
~Napoleon Hill

I am dedicating this chapter to all of the people who are afraid to fall off the skateboard. By now, I have shared with you some very personal falls I have taken. I would like to switch the emphasis from the falls outside of your control that cause pain to the pain you cause yourself by being afraid to try something new.

We get stuck. Mostly we get stuck in our routines because they become convenient. We are not afraid when we know what to expect. Then we wonder why we are bored. It's because we continue the same tasks everyday. People have music inside their hearts but to pursue that music causes them to do something different. It's scary to do something new. In a live lecture, Dr. Leo Buscaglia said, "How am I different? And if you find out night after night you are not different, then jump out the window, run around the block and when the cops stop you, you say you are doing something different." That's great wisdom.

So what are you afraid of? Are you afraid that you might be wrong? Leo goes on and says, "You know a clock that stopped is right twice a day." That's classic. There is nothing wrong with being wrong.

Are you afraid of failure? I love that word because I haven't used it since school. Dr. Wayne Dyer said that there's no such thing as failure. Everything you do produces results. You put a golf ball on a tee and try to hit it. So what if you don't hit it 300 yards. You hit it 25 yards. You have not failed, you have produced some results. I love when Thomas Edison was asked how did it feel to have failed when he attempted 10,000 ways to make a battery work. He simply replied, "Fail, I haven't failed. I just produced 10,000 ways on how <u>not</u> to make a battery work. What have you done?" The key here is what have you done?

Failure is a concept that you can use and abuse all day long. It's up to you. I am telling you that your success in school or at work will be dependent upon how well you persevere and are willing to try new things. That's how people become great. Elvis shook his legs and gyrated on a stage. People thought he was weird, but he was doing something different. That's the key.

I have an exercise you can do right now. I want you to close your eyes and visualize yourself about 80 years old and sitting on a rocking chair on your porch. Once you have that image, I want you to see yourself rocking back and forth. Do that a few times. Now, close your eyes and go back to a time when you were the age you are now reading this book. As an 80 year old ask yourself what would you have tried differently back then? What would you have been willing to try? What was the music inside your heart back then but you were too scared to pursue? Now open your eyes.

Here you are presently sitting, standing, or laying down. That 80 year old sent you a message. You will be old one day. You will be sitting somewhere someday reminiscing about the past. You have a chance right now to try that thing you are so afraid of. If it doesn't work out then you will know now. Then you can move on. It's a series of events that you have control over right now. Don't miss it. It could be the music that changes the world, and most importantly, yourself. Go and be better than you used to be.

SUGGESTIONS & REVIEW

"Life is either a daring adventure or nothing."
~Helen Keller

(THE CAMEL) I learned that **forgiveness** was the only path for me to take so I could move on and be productive in my life.

My suggestion for you is to find that person who has wronged you and in your mind has kept you from reaching your potential. Understand that it is the way you react to this person that causes you the pain. Now use forgiveness so you can move on and take control of your life.

*Notes:*_____

_____

_____

_____

(SCROOGE IS ON TV AGAIN) I learned that admitting that I had this pain in my heart helped me tremendously. I regained my life back by talking to someone who helped me work through this experience.

My suggestion for you is to stop being the victim and understand there is no reason to blame yourself. Take responsibility by talking to someone. As time goes on, forgiveness will be a major key to your well-being. Forgiveness is probably one of the most powerful ways you can move forward and make your life beautiful.

*Notes:*_____

_____

_____

_____

(THANK YOU FOR SPENDING YOUR TIME THINKING ABOUT ME)
Gandhi said, "No one can hurt me without my permission."
I realized that I can't control what people do or say. I also
changed my thinking about the situation.

My suggestion for you is the next time someone is not kind
to you, know that they have to do that in order to feel better about themselves. It's almost always never about you.
Keep the focus on what's good and keep it off of why they
are mean, etc. What happens is that you will waste a lot of
time and come up with a list of their faults.

*Notes:*_____
_____
_____
_____

(THE DAY THE LIGHTS WENT OUT) I really try to live my life
without regrets. I make sure that when I am talking to
someone on the phone I always end with "I love you". I
have a philosophy that you never know, so I want to just
make sure I have communicated those three little words
that are powerful and magical.

My suggestion for you is to live a life with no regrets. Tell
the people you care about that you love them. Do goofy
things like write them unexpected letters and put them in
the most unusual places such as under their pillow or in
the refrigerator. Hug the people you love.

*Notes:*_____
_____
_____
_____

(VICTOR, IT'S TUCCI) I learned to take the initiative and open my mouth and say hello. You never know who you will meet. I also learned that believing in something can lead to great things. People do what they do given the circumstances of their lives. I learned to not take things so personally.

My suggestion for you is to put yourself out there and knock on the doors that really ring true for you. When the door closes, knock some more. Be humble by not thinking you are entitled to something.

Notes:_____

_____

_____

_____

(THE COURAGE OF A LION) I cried when my sister died. I cried when my brother-in-law died. I think crying is a great way to heal. It seems painful at the time you are doing it, but it's a wonderful thing to do. It took some time but I decided that I couldn't live a life in pain all of the time so I began asking "What can I do to make a difference?"

My suggestion for you is to make a difference. If you can, be there for others when something tragic happens. The most important thing I can tell you is don't be afraid to cry.

Notes:_____

_____

_____

_____

(MY THOUGHTS ARE THE OBSTACLE) It's not the obstacle itself that causes the upset, it's your thoughts about the obstacle itself. Once again, I am learning that people do what they do given the circumstances of their lives. It doesn't mean it's right or wrong. How you process it is up to you.

My suggestion for you is to be aware of the next time you get upset and mad at someone. Try to respond and not react.

*Notes:*_____

_____

_____

_____

(CHOOSE KINDNESS) I have learned to take my blinders off more regularly. Many times we go through our day and focus so much on ourselves that we don't look around and see what's going on around us. I developed The Neysaké Foundation. It is my hope that each year I host this benefit to raise more money than the year before.

My suggestion for you is to be more aware when you have your blinders on. The next time you are out just look around and see if someone needs help. It could be as simple as holding a door open. Little acts of kindness go a long way in the hearts of others.

*Notes:*_____

_____

_____

_____

(TRUE NOBILITY) It is the theme of this book. I am better today than I was yesterday by being more self-confident. I was talking to people last night about what I do for a living and I was able to speak from a genuine and confident place. It was awesome!

My suggestion for you is to wake up tomorrow and answer this question: How am I better today than I was yesterday? It may help to put a piece of paper next to your bed tonight to jot down your response.

*Notes:*_____

_____

_____

_____

(NOT BEHIND A COMPUTER) What is that something you are excited about that keeps you from going to sleep at night? For me, it's the book I am writing or it's my upcoming presentation. I can guarantee that if I was still sitting behind a computer designing a car ad, I would be emotionally drained.

My suggestion for you is to not take my word for it. What works for me may not for you. However, if there is something that excites you and keeps you up at night, then you should probably listen to your heart. Whad'ya think?

*Notes:*_____

_____

_____

_____

(MR. P, CAN I SING WITH YOU?) I learned that my true music was in me all of the time. I just needed help from some friends to get it out. I opened my mind up to all kinds of possibilities. By doing that, I am living my passion today. I get to travel and inspire people of all ages. I am so grateful that little Matt came into my life and taught me this lesson.

My suggestion for you is to have an open mind when it comes to your true music. Understand that everything that has happened to you in the past has led you to this point in your life.

Notes:_____

_____

_____

_____

(I AM READY TO GO ON TOUR) I learned it's remarkable to have dreams. It's even more remarkable to follow through as much as possible to make those dreams come true. It's beyond remarkable when your immediate dream doesn't come true because your destiny is waiting for you.

My suggestion for you is to re-read the "Lucky Penny" analogy. When things don't work out the way you planned, learn the lesson and grow from there. Don't feel sorry for yourself.

Notes:_____

_____

_____

_____

(A NIGHT FOR RENEÉ) It's amazing to me that so many people have stepped up to help women in need. For me, it's been an incredible journey. Before my sister, I didn't really pay much attention to women that needed help. I have taken off my blinders and it has made a world of difference.

My suggestion for you is to help someone in need. If there's something close to your heart then do something that could make a difference. All it takes is a little energy on your part.

Notes:_____

_____

_____

_____

(THE PUNCH THAT SAVED MY LIFE) Everything happens for a reason. I may not have known the reason right away but I know it to be true. I really believe that the punch did save my life. It taught me to be more respectful of people. Now I can help children and make better choices when it comes to treating all people with dignity, respect, and kindness.

My suggestion for you is see where you can find how this way of thinking has been true for you. What are the reasons that your life is where it is today?

Notes:_____

_____

_____

_____

(IMPOSSIBLE) At this stage of the game, anytime I view something as impossible, I begin to look at the problem and start asking some different kinds of questions. For example, this is not going to work turns to what am I overlooking here that could make it work? Or is there another option that could work? What can I do differently that could make the difference?

My suggestion for you is to take a potential problem you have right now and start asking different questions. If you believe that you are not good enough at something, I ask you to look at the word "Impossible" and then change it around to "I'm Possible." Remember, it's the same letters. I am asking you to look at changing your thoughts.

Notes:_____
_____
_____
_____

(THE ROCKING CHAIR) This is one my favorite exercises because it really puts things in perspective. It makes me realize that life is short and you have to make the best of what you have. There is an old saying "Live today like it's the first day of the rest of your life." I look at it this way, "Live today like it's the last day of your life." We never know.

My suggestion for you is to live with a sense of excitement every day. Do something different!

Notes:_____
_____
_____
_____

FROM SNOW CONES TO MICROPHONES

"I learned very early in life that: "Without a song, the day would never end; without a song, a man ain't got a friend; without a song, the road would never bend— without a song." So I keep singing a song."
~Elvis Presley

We have many things in common. One thing is for sure is that we were all children once. I was eight when I took the microphone for the first time. I haven't let go in 29 years.

Music is a great way to express your feelings. I have written many songs that demonstrate how to overcome the skateboard. The following pages feature lyrics and poems ranging from songs I have recorded and performed to songs I have yet to record.

I looked up the word music and this is what the dictionary said, "Music is an art of sound in time that expresses ideas and emotions in significant forms through the elements of rhythm, melody, harmony, and color." Isn't that what life is all about?

MY DREAMS

I WANT TO TAKE YOU ON A JOURNEY.
IT ALL STARTS INSIDE OF YOU.
CLOSE YOUR EYES AND VISUALIZE
ALL THE THINGS THAT YOU CAN DO.
LIKE A LION IN THE JUNGLE
OR AND EAGLE IN THE SKY.
YOUR POSSIBILITIES ARE ENDLESS
YOU'RE FREE TO ROAM AND TRY.

I BELIEVE IN MYSELF
THERE'S NOTHING I CAN'T DO.
FOLLOW MY DREAMS
I'LL MAKE THEM COME TRUE.
NO MATTER WHAT PEOPLE WANT ME TO BE
MY DREAMS ARE MY DREAMS AND
NO ONE CAN TAKE THEM FROM ME.

HERE NO EVIL, SPEAK NO EVIL, TELL NO LIES
YOU'LL SHINE LIKE THE BRIGHTEST STAR IN THE SKY
BE HONEST WITH YOURSELF AND YOU WILL FLY
YOU'RE BOUNDED BY NOTHING
LET ME TELL YOU WHY.

YOU DON'T HAVE TO TRAVEL VERY FAR
TO SEE AND REALIZE HOW SPECIAL YOU ARE.
YOUR DESTINATION IS INSIDE YOUR HEART
LET IT GUIDE YOU, MOTIVATE YOU, INSPIRE YOU.

SHE'S HERE TO STAY (I SANG THIS AT MY MOTHER'S FUNERAL)

THERE ARE NO BRIGHT LIGHTS IN VEGAS TODAY.
MY NUMBER ONE PRIZE WAS TAKEN AWAY.
THIS PYRAMID WILL NEVER SEE
ANOTHER SUNSET SO PEACEFULLY.

SOURING ABOVE I CAN'T EXPLAIN.
A BLINK OF AN EYE IT STARTS TO RAIN.
THIS RAIN MAY SEEM LIKE DEATH,
IT'S AS PEACEFUL AS HER FIRST BREATH.

CAN YOU HEAR THE BELLS, THEY WILL RING
ALL THE CHILDREN WILL PLAY AND SING.
TOUCH THE RAIN, IT WILL BE OK,
DON'T BE AFRAID SHE'S HERE TO STAY.

I'LL HOLD A FLOWER IN MY HAND
SIT UNDER A TREE OR PLAY IN THE SAND.
SHE'S WITH ME ANY TIME OF DAY,
LIFE'S NOT MADE OF STONES IT'S MADE OF CLAY.

LISTEN TO YOUR HEART WHAT DOES IT SAY?
YOU HAVE IT IN YOU TO MAKE YOUR WAY.
SHE TOOK A PATH THAT WAS PAVED IN GOLD.
SHE WAS LOVED BY ALL THEY BROKE THE MOLD.

CAN YOU HEAR THE BELLS, THEY WILL RING
ALL THE CHILDREN WILL PLAY AND SING.
TOUCH THE RAIN, IT WILL BE OK, DON'T BE AFRAID,
SHE'S HERE TO STAY.

I CLOSE MY EYES, AND SHE IS THERE
SHE'S IN HEAVEN, THERE'S NOTHING TO FEAR.
TOUCH THE RAIN, IT WILL BE OK
DON'T BE AFRAID SHE'S HERE TO STAY.

NO PLACE FOR A MOTHER'S DAY

A CEMETERY IS NO PLACE FOR A MOTHER'S DAY.
BUT I HAVE NO OTHER CHOICE.
I MISS YOU, I SEE YOU
I CAN HEAR YOUR VOICE.

AS I LOOK BACK ON THESE DAYS
I SMILE, FOR YOU GAVE ME LIFE.
YOU DESERVED EVERYDAY
TO BE A MOTHER'S DAY.

WHAT CAN I SAY ABOUT THIS DAY
AS I LOOK AT YOUR NAME.
THE THOUGHTS ARE ONLY GOOD ONES
BUT THE PARTIES WON'T BE THE SAME.

TO ME, THIS DAY IS JUST ANOTHER DAY
WITH A DRESS AND A SUIT ON DISPLAY.
EVERY MORNING, EVERY NIGHT
IS THE WAY TO CELEBRATE A MOTHER'S LIFE.

BECAUSE NO ONE KNOWS
WHAT TOMORROW HOLDS.
TODAY IS TRULY THE ONLY DAY.
SO I SAY TO ALL THE WOMEN
I KNOW MY MOM IS WITH ME.
WHEN YOU SMILE OR KISS YOUR CHILD HELLO.
I'LL STAND BACK AND ENJOY ALL THE LOVE.

LUCKY PENNY

FOUND A PENNY ON THE GROUND
IT WAS SHINY AND SO ROUND.

I PICKED THAT PENNY OFF THE GROUND
AND PUT IT IN MY POCKET AND ALL DAY LONG.

MY WISHES CAME TRUE THE SKY WAS BLUE
THE SUN WAS SHINING BECAUSE OF YOU.

OH LUCKY PENNY TAKE MY HAND.
I HAVE A SONG TO SING THROUGHOUT THIS LAND.
FROM SCHOOL TO SCHOOL FROM MILE TO MILE
I WANT HER TO LAUGH, I WANT HIM TO SMILE.

FOUND YOU ROLLING AROUND TODAY
I LOOKED UP IN THE SKY WHAT COULD I SAY.

MADE MY WISH BUT THIS TIME GAVE YOU A RIDE.
YOU LANDED BY THE KIDS ON THE PLAYGROUND SLIDE.

OH LUCKY PENNY TAKE THEIR HAND.
THEY HAVE A SONG TO SING THROUGHOUT THIS LAND.
FROM SCHOOL TO SCHOOL FROM MILE TO MILE.
THEY MAKE ME LAUGH, THEY MAKE ME SMILE.

THE ROCKING CHAIR (WRITTEN FOR YOU)

IN A LITTLE TOWN ALONG A WINDING STREAM
LIVED A GRAY HAIRED MAN WHO LIVED HIS DREAM.

HE'S ROCKING ALONG WITH BOTH EYES CLOSED
REMINISCING OF THE PAST AND OF THE PATH HE CHOSE.

HE HAD SOME STRUGGLES HE HAD TO MAKE SOME CHOICES, BUT HE WOULD
CATCH HIMSELF LISTENING TO ALL OF THOSE UNFORGETTABLE VOICES.

BUT THROUGH IT ALL, WITH RESPECT AND ADMIRATION
HIS VOICE RANG THE LOUDEST IT WAS THE SECRET TO HIS DESTINATION.

HE ROCKED ALONG SWAYING FROM PATH TO PATH
HE MADE SAME MISTAKES BUT HE NEVER LOOKED BACK.
HE ROCKED ALONG FROM YEAR TO YEAR
WITH SOME GREAT TIMES AND SOME PRETTY SAD TEARS.

BUT NOW LATE IN HIS LIFE HE SPENDS LESS TIME IN THE CHAIR
WITH A SMILE ON HIS FACE HE LEANED AND WHISPERED IN MY EAR.

I HAVE A SECRET TO SHARE SO LISTEN AND LEARN,
WHEN YOU REACH YOUR CROSSROAD IT COULD BE THE DIFFERENCE OF
STAYING STRAIGHT OR TAKING THAT TURN.

VISUALIZE YOURSELF OLD AND GRAY LIKE ME.
PUT YOURSELF IN THE CHAIR CLOSE YOUR EYES AND YOU WILL SEE.

THAT THING YOU WERE AFRAID TO TRY OR THAT THING YOU WERE AFRAID TO
SAY, WILL YOU REGRET IT WHEN YOU'RE OLD SOMEDAY?

IF THE ANSWER IS YES WHICH I THINK IT WILL BE, YOU'RE YOUNG ENOUGH TO
MAKE THAT CHANGE AND REALIZE WHO YOU WANT TO BE.

I CLOSED MY EYES AND ROCKED LIKE I WAS 83
THIS WAS THE DAY I BEGAN TO SEE THE SECRET HE TOLD ME.

THE ARTIST WITHIN

ONCE UPON A TIME IN A KINGDOM FAR AWAY
LIVED A SPECIAL KIND OF KID, HIS NAME WAS LITTLE SID.
HIS EYES COULD SEE BEYOND THE TREASURES OF THE LAND
GRATEFUL FOR WHAT HE HAD, BUT PREFERRED TO GIVE A HAND.

NO MAGIC KINGDOM, NO KING OR QUEEN,
NO FANCY LABEL, NO LIMOUSINE.
NO SUPERSTAR, NO FANCY DRESS.
CAN GIVE YOU ANY HAPPINESS.

HE STRUGGLED AND TRIED TO BE LIKE ALL HIS FRIENDS
TO GO WITH THE FLOW AND FOLLOW THE TRENDS.
INTO THE FOREST HE WALKED AND MET A FRIENDLY FACE
LISTEN TO THESE WORDS AND SEE WHAT YOU CAN BE.

THE SECRET YOU WILL FIND IS IN YOUR HEART AND SOUL
NO MATTER WHERE YOU GO NO MATTER WHERE YOU GO.
NO SUPERSTAR, NO FANCY DRESS
CAN GIVE YOU ANY HAPPINESS.

THE ARTIST WITHIN IS WHERE IT WILL BEGIN
YOU WILL SEE WHAT YOU CAN BE.
YOU HAVE THE POWER TO INSPIRE THE FIRE INSIDE.
JUST IMAGINE IF YOU TRY IMAGINE IF YOU TRY.

AS THE FRIENDLY FACE DISAPPEARED THROUGH THE TREES
LITTLE SID WITH A SMILE FELL TO HIS KNEES
THE KEY IS INSIDE, INSIDE OF YOU AND ME.
NO MATTER WHERE YOU GO, NO MATTER WHERE YOU GO.

NO MAGIC KINGDOM, NO KING OR QUEEN,
NO FANCY LABEL, NO LIMOUSINE.
NO SUPERSTAR, NO FANCY DRESS
CAN GIVE YOU ANY HAPPINESS.

MOMENTS WITH YOU (WRITTEN FOR MY WIFE BRENDA)

SITTIN' ON THE BEACH, WATCHIN' THE SUN GO DOWN.
HOLDING HANDS AS WE WALK ACROSS THE TOWN.
WATCHIN' A PLAY, TELLING ME YOUR STORY
SHARING A BOTTLE OF WINE, IT'S GETTING TO BE THAT TIME.

ALL WE HAVE IS PARADISE IN OUR HEARTS
EXCHANGING AND ARRANGING AS WE GET OUR FRESH NEW START.
LIKE CINDERELLA YOUR SMILE HAS TAKEN MY HEART
FROM THE POND TO THIS DAY, A PRINCE LIVIN' A FAIRY TALE.

MOMENT TO MOMENT
SHARING A KISS, SHARING A LAUGH AND MAKING A WISH.
MOMENT TO MOMENT
BELIEVING IN YOU BELIEVING IN ME THIS WISH CAME TRUE
MOMENT TO MOMENT LEADS TO ANOTHER MOMENT WITH YOU.

TAKING A MOPED RIDE, ADMIRING YOUR BACK SIDE
AS I FOLLOW YOU ALONG THE WINDING ROAD.
A KISS ON THE CHEEK, A HUG JUST BECAUSE I FEEL LIKE IT
NOON OR NIGHT WRONG OR RIGHT IT'S OK IT WILL BE ALL RIGHT.

LIKE THAT BOTTLE, WE GET BETTER WITH AGE
GROWING WISER AND OLDER TOGETHER WILL BE OUR STAGE.
THE LIGHTS WILL KEEP ON SHINING AND WILL NEVER GO DIM...EVEN WHEN
THE CURTAIN CLOSES I CAN PROMISE YOU THIS...MY MOMENTS WITH YOU
WILL NEVER DIE IN THIS LIFETIME OR THE NEXT.

MOMENT TO MOMENT
SHARING A KISS, SHARING A LAUGH & MAKING A WISH.
MOMENT TO MOMENT
BELIEVING IN YOU BELIEVING IN ME THIS WISH CAME TRUE
MOMENT TO MOMENT LEADS TO ANOTHER MOMENT WITH YOU.

I'M POSSIBLE

A LITTLE BOY
MAKING HIS WAY
WONDERIN' WHAT TO DO.
HE SAW A SIGN FOR A CHANCE TO PLAY BALL
BUT HE THOUGHT HE WASN'T GOOD AT ALL.

HE SAID,
IT'S IMPOSSIBLE
I CAN'T DO THAT.
PEOPLE WILL LAUGH AT ME.
HE SAID,
IT'S IMPOSSIBLE
I CAN'T DO THAT.
PEOPLE WILL LAUGH AT ME.

A LITTLE GIRL
MAKING HER WAY
WONDERIN' WHAT TO DO.
SHE SAW A SIGN FOR A CHANCE TO DANCE
BUT HER SMILE TURNED UPSIDE DOWN.

SHE SAID,
IT'S IMPOSSIBLE
I CAN'T DO THAT
PEOPLE WILL LAUGH AT ME.
SHE SAID,
IT'S IMPOSSIBLE
I CAN'T DO THAT
PEOPLE WILL LAUGH AT ME.

THEN ONE DAY
THEY HEARD SOMEONE SAY.
ALL YOU HAVE TO DO
IS LOOK AT IT THIS WAY...

CHANGE THE WAY
YOU LOOK AT THINGS
AND THE THINGS YOU LOOK
AT CHANGE.

CUZ,
I'M POSSIBLE.
I CAN DO THAT
I WANT TO FEEL GOOD
AT THIS OR THAT.
ALL I KNOW IT'S REALLY TRUE
I CAN DO THAT
CUZ I'M POSSIBLE
I CAN DO THAT
CUZ I'M POSSIBLE.

A LESSON IN SESSION

FROM THE PLAYGROUND
MONDAY AFTERNOON,
BELLS ARE RINGING,
CHILDREN JUMPING,
RUNNING, PLAYING, BEING WHAT MOST OF US WANT TO BE.

A LINE FOR THE SLIDE
4-SQUARE GAMES,
SWINGS ARE SWINGING,
CHILDREN SINGING, HIDING,
SEEKING, SEEING WHAT MOST DON'T SEE.

PICTURE PERFECT MOMENT
CHILDREN BEING CHILDREN,
NO JUDGMENTS, NO DENIALS, MILES AND MILES
OF LAUGHING AND PLAYING

PICTURE PERFECT MOMENT
CHILDREN BEING CHILDREN,
NO JUDGMENTS, NO DENIALS, MILES AND MILES
OF LAUGHING AND PLAYING

JOHNNY'S WALKING
BY HIMSELF
FEELS ALONE
KELLY'S PLAYING,
LOOKING, NOTICING,
LEAVES HER GAME TO BE WITH HIM.

HEY JOHNNY
WHAT'S THE MATTER?
MY DAD IS LEAVING
KELLY'S LISTENING
JOHNNY'S CRYING,
KELLY HUGS JOHNNY'S TEARS AWAY.

PICTURE PERFECT MOMENT
CHILDREN BEING CHILDREN,
NO JUDGMENTS, NO DENIALS, A LESSON
IN SESSION FOR EVERY GROWN UP TO SEE.

PICTURE PERFECT MOMENT
CHILDREN BEING CHILDREN,
NO JUDGMENTS, NO DENIALS, A LESSON
IN SESSION FOR EVERY GROWN UP TO SEE.

FERRIS WHEEL

I'M SITTIN' ON THE WHEEL AS IT GOES ROUND AND ROUND
WONDERIN' WHERE MY LIFE WILL TAKE ME.
MY LIFE IS A CIRCLE OF HOPES AND DREAMS
I'M SEARCHIN' FOR THE ANSWER WITHIN ME.

LET THE WHEEL TAKE CONTROL IS EASY TO DO
MOVING ME THROUGH THE MOTIONS OF LIFE.
IT'S TIME TO WAKE UP, TIME TO TAKE A CHANCE
CHANGE MY DIRECTION, TAKE A DIFFERENT PATH.

FERRIS WHEEL, FERRIS WHEEL, ROUND AND ROUND
YOU'VE GIVEN ME THE SAME OLD LOOKS AND THE SAME OLD SOUNDS.
IT'S TIME FOR A DIFFERENT RIDE PERHAPS THAT BANANA SLIDE.

YOU CAN'T DO IT, DON'T EVEN TRY.
THESE ARE WORDS I NO LONGER LIVE BY.
I'M NOT INTIMIDATED, DON'T YOU SEE,
IF I FALL OR SOMEONE PUSHES, IT WON'T STOP ME.

I'VE OPENED MY EYES AND NOW I SEE
THAT MY DREAMS ARE IN MY REACH.
I HAVE PLACES TO GO, WAYS TO GROW
THIS IS NOT A DRESS REHEARSAL, THIS IS THE SHOW.

FERRIS WHEEL FERRIS WHEEL ROUND AND ROUND
YOU'VE GIVEN ME THE SAME OLD LOOKS AND THE SAME OLD SOUNDS.
IT'S TIME FOR A DIFFERENT RIDE PERHAPS THAT BANANA SLIDE.

THE TORNADO (WRITTEN ABOUT MY DAD)

A CHILD CAN SEES SO MANY THINGS
A VISION WITHOUT LIMITS.
EARS AND EYES BECOME THESE POWERFUL MAGNETS.

THE INNOCENCE, LIKE A BIRD IN FLIGHT
ALWAYS TRYIN', BUT SOMETIMES CRYIN'
BEING PULLED BY THE WIND OF A FAMILY.

INSTEAD OF WAKING UP TO THE SOUNDS
OF MORNING AND SUN IT'S THE MIDDLE OF THE NIGHT
AND HE'S ON THE RUN.

HIS BODY IS HERE STRENGTH OF A HUNDRED LIONS
BUT HIS MIND IS IN THE BOTTLE
ONCE AGAIN, I WAKE UP CRYING.

YELLING LIKE THUNDER, QUICK TAKE COVER
THE TORNADO HAS STARTED AGAIN
TAKE MY HAND, HE'LL SUCK YOU IN
TO HIS EMPTY AND UNPREDICTABLE WORLD.

SO MANY NIGHTS OF THUNDERSTORMS
HE WHIRLED AND TWIRLED FROM CHILD TO CHILD
PLACING BLAME FOR HIS UNCONTROLLABLE WINDS.

THERE WERE SOME OBSTACLES
THAT CAME ALONG HIS WAY A GLIMMER OF HOPE
THE BEAMING SUNSHINE OF A MOTHER.

SHE WAS NO MATCH FOR HIM
HE TWISTED HIS WAY RIGHT THROUGH
IT ALWAYS RAINED BUT NOT FROM THE SKY
THESE WERE TEARS FROM THE CHILDREN'S INNOCENT EYES.

A NIGHTMARE REMAINED
THROUGH THE CHILDREN'S SPECIAL DAYS
THE MEMORIES LINGER
OF A TORNADO THAT GOT HIS WAY.

THERE WAS A TIME WHEN THIS MAN GOT SCARED
THE SUN SHINED UPON HIM
AS THE TORNADO DISAPPEARED.

YELLING LIKE THUNDER, QUICK TAKE COVER
THE TORNADO HAS STARTED AGAIN.
TAKE MY HAND, HE'LL SUCK YOU IN
TO HIS EMPTY AND UNPREDICTABLE WORLD.

THE DAY THE LIGHTS WENT OUT (WRITTEN FOR MY MOM)

AS I SIT IN THIS HOTEL ROOM
A PEN IN MY HAND.
A DESERT BEFORE ME
MILES AND MILES OF SAND.

I FEEL MY TIME HAS COME
MY TASK AT HAND IS COMPLETE.
I'M GOING TO TRAVEL THIS DESSERT AND SEE
THE OTHER HORIZONS OUT THERE FOR ME.

I WRITE YOU THIS NOTE
BECAUSE YOU KNOW ME BY NOW
MY WORDS ARE TRUE,
REMEMBER, MY SON, EVEN FROM VEGAS, I MISS YOU!

THE DAY THE LIGHTS WENT OUT BLACKJACK BY CANDLELIGHT
SINGERS, DANCERS TAKE STAGE RIGHT
C'MON LUCKY SEVEN DON'T LET ME DOWN
NO MATTER WHAT, THE SHOW MUST GO ON.

I MAY BE OUT OF YOUR SIGHT
BUT I NEVER WILL LEAVE YOUR SIDE.
I WILL SHOW UP IN OTHER WAYS
I'M COMING ALONG FOR THE RIDE.

LOOK UP IN THAT SKY
DID YOU RECOGNIZE THAT STAR?
A FRIEND HE WILL BECOME
YOU WILL SEE HIM FROM A FAR.

A SMILE WILL GREET YOU
A KINDNESS WILL WARM THE AIR.
A GUARDIAN ANGEL OF SORTS
UNCOMMON AND UNLIKELY, BUT HE WILL CARE,
EVEN FROM VEGAS, I MISS YOU!

THE DAY THE LIGHTS WENT OUT
BLACKJACK BY CANDLELIGHT
SINGERS, DANCERS TAKE STAGE RIGHT
C'MON LUCKY SEVEN DON'T LET ME DOWN
NO MATTER WHAT, THE SHOW MUST GO ON.

THREE ANGELS

IF I LIVED BACK IN '23
YOU KNOW THERE'S SOMEONE I'D LIKE TO MEET.
HE FOUGHT FOR FREEDOM AND HE USED HIS VOICE
AS THE ONLY WEAPON OF HIS CHOICE.

HE REACHED AND TEACHED AND HE SAID OUT LOUD
THAT FIGHTING MAKES NO SENSE.
HE TRAVELED AND UNRAVELED WORDS OF PEACE.
HE NEVER EVER GAVE UP.

OH GANDHI, GANDHI
WHEREVER YOU ARE
GIVE US A SIGN TELL US YOU'RE FINE.
I CAN HEAR HIM SAYIN' TO YOU AND ME THAT
THERE'S A WORLD OF HOPE AND A WORLD OF PEACE.
BUT IT STARTS WITH A SMILE FROM YOU AND ME.

IF I LIVED BACK IN '53
YOU KNOW THERE'S SOMEONE I'D LIKE TO MEET.
HE FOUGHT FOR EQUALITY DAY AND NIGHT
HE KNEW DEEP DOWN WHAT WAS RIGHT.

HE PREACHED AND HE TEACHED AND HE SAID OUT LOUD
THAT PREJUDICE MAKES NO SENSE.
HE TRAVELED AND UNRAVELED WORDS OF PEACE
HE NEVER EVER GAVE UP.

OH MARTIN, MARTIN
WHEREVER YOU ARE
GIVE US A SIGN TELL US YOU'RE FINE.
I CAN HEAR HIM SAYIN' TO YOU AND ME THAT
THERE'S A WORLD OF HOPE AND A WORLD OF PEACE.
BUT IT STARTS WITH A SMILE FROM YOU AND ME.

IF I LIVED BACK IN '63
YOU KNOW THERE'S A WOMAN I'D LIKE TO MEET.
THIS WOMAN WAS DETERMINED TO GIVE A HAND
AND HELP A CHILD A WOMAN AND A MAN.

SHE WALKED AND TALKED AND SAID OUT LOUD
IF YOU WANT TO HELP YOU HAVE TO SHOW SOME LOVE.
SHE TRAVELED AND UNRAVELED WORDS OF PEACE
SHE NEVER EVER GAVE UP.

OH MOTHER TERESA WHEREVER YOU ARE
GIVE US A SIGN TELL US YOU'RE FINE.
I CAN HEAR HER SAYIN' TO YOU AND ME THAT
THERE'S A WORLD OF HOPE AND A WORLD OF PEACE
BUT IT STARTS WITH A SMILE FROM YOU AND ME.

LITTLE RED WAGON JUMPIN' JACK

A LITTLE RED WAGON
PASSING BY
I HAPPEN TO SEE IT
FROM THE CORNER OF MY EYE.

I'D JUMP ON HANG ON
WHEN I WAS EIGHT
DINNERS READY
I WAS ALWAYS LATE.

STOPPED FOR A MOMENT
WHAT SHOULD I DO
I'M A GROWN UP, GROWIN' UP
TO BE A KID AGAIN.

LITTLE RED WAGON JUMPIN' JACK
LET'S GO FOR A RIDE TO THE CORNER AND BACK
PUSH UP, SIT UP, I'M FIVE AGAIN
LITTLE RED WAGON JUMPIN' JACK.

THERE'S A SMILE IN THERE
I KNOW I CAN
TOO SERIOUS, IT'S HILARIOUS
I WANT TO BE A KID AGAIN.

I'M TAKIN' THE DAY
TO SMILE AGAIN
A GROWN UP, LOOSEN UP
AND BE A KID AGAIN.

LITTLE RED WAGON JUMPIN' JACK
LET'S GO FOR A RIDE TO THE CORNER AND BACK
PUSH UP, SIT UP, SIX AGAIN
LITTLE RED WAGON JUMPIN' JACK.

LITTLE RED WAGON JUMPIN' JACK
LET'S GO FOR A RIDE TO THE CORNER AND BACK
PUSH UP, SIT UP, SEVEN AGAIN
LITTLE RED WAGON JUMPIN' JACK.

IT'S OK TO CRY

DID YOU EVER SIT ON THE BEACH
AND MAKE A SAND CASTLE AS THE SUN SETS FOR THE DAY.
WHEN YOU RETURN YOU SEE THAT THE OCEAN
THE OCEAN TOOK IT ALL AWAY.

YOU LOOK TO THE LEFT, YOU LOOK TO THE RIGHT
BUT THERE'S NOT A SOUL IN SIGHT.
YOUR EYES BEGIN TO TEAR
BUT THERE'S NOTHING TO FEAR, EVERYTHING WILL BE ALL RIGHT.

IT'S OK TO CRY
WHEN YOU HAVE TO SAY GOODBYE
JUST LISTEN TO THE OCEAN SOUND.
AS THE TRUTH UNFOLDS FROM YOUR VERY SOUL
NEVER LOST BUT ALWAYS FOUND.

YOU WILL SEE I AM SURE ONE DAY
THAT IT WAS YOUR VERY TEAR THAT WASHED YOUR CASTLE AWAY.
YOU AND WHAT YOU LOVE WILL NEVER PART
IT WILL ALWAYS BE FOUND IN YOUR BEATING HEART.

IT'S OK TO CRY
WHEN YOU HAVE TO SAY GOODBYE
JUST LISTEN TO THE OCEAN SOUND.
AS THE TRUTH UNFOLDS FROM YOUR VERY SOUL
NEVER LOST BUT ALWAYS FOUND.

MAGICLAND (FOR MY MIMMI)

THROUGH THE DOOR, UNDER THE STAIRS
THERE'S A PLACE THAT WE CAN GO.
WHERE YOU CAN RIDE THE HORSE, DANCE OF COURSE,
OR WATCH YOUR FAVORITE FLOWER GROW.

THROUGH THE DOOR, UNDER THE STAIRS
THERE'S PLACE THAT WE CAN GO.
YOU CAN SING YOUR FAVORITE SONG ALL DAY LONG,
OR MAKE YOUR FAVORITE BUILDING GROW.

LET'S GO TO MAGICLAND, MAGICLAND
IMAGINE WHAT YOU CAN DO.
LET'S GO TO MAGICLAND, MAGICLAND
IT'S YOU AND ME, AND ME AND YOU.

IT'S RAINBOWS, IT'S STORY TIME,
IT'S DANCING TO SONGS THAT RHYME.
IT'S COOK YOUR FAVORITE DISH
IT'S CLOSE YOUR EYES, MAKE A WISH
IT'S MAGICLAND, IT'S MAGICLAND, C'MON TAKE MY HAND.

THROUGH THE DOOR, UNDER THE STAIRS
THERE'S A PLACE THAT WE CAN GO.
I CAN BE TEN, ELEVEN, TWELVE AGAIN,
AND I CAN WATCH YOU AS YOU GROW.

LET'S GO TO MAGICLAND, MAGICLAND
IMAGINE WHAT YOU CAN DO.
LET'S GO TO MAGICLAND, MAGICLAND
IT'S YOU AND ME, AND ME AND YOU.

ABOUT THE AUTHOR

Victor is the founder of Childhood Victories, Inc and is the author of *Winning Within, There's Only One You, Be Seen and Heard, Your VOICE, My Dreams,* and has recorded two music CD's. Not only is he a survivor of sexual abuse but his sister was murdered in 2001 by her husband. He co-founded A Night For Reneé, an annual benefit that raises money and awareness for domestic violence. He has raised over $300,000 for WINGS (Domestic Violence Agency). After working with over 800,000 children and countless adults, Victor has created a framework that radically shifts old paradigms and helps people overcome their adversity so they can live successful and happy lives.

Victor caught the inspirational eye of Dr. Wayne Dyer and was asked to sing during his Power of Intention tour. Wayne said, "Victor, you did a great job with my audience. My granddaughter loved your book."

Victor delivers the "WOW" factor audiences want and the essential content that schools/organizations are looking for. His programs are a balance of high-energy, humor, and thought provoking moments. His interactive format incorporates music and a variety of multi-media approaches. He creates an experience where people walk away with an increased positive self-regard and improved outlook on life. His clients have included the Illinois PTA, Kansas PTA, Indiana PTA, National PTA, Abbott Labs, WINGS, and schools all across the country.

For booking inquiries call ████████
or visit www.VictorPacini.com

Dynamic Presentations and Products that Inspire and Captivate!

Victor's Erin's Law Program
Be Seen and Heard©

"I thought Victor was fantastic. He did a great job sharing a very uncomfortable message. His book was well written and well presented and it was great that he offered a free download to all of the families - great way to start a conversation at home."

Teacher, Northbrook School District 28

Books and Audios

FROM VICTIM TO VICTOR
5 AUDIO TRANSFORMATIONAL SESSIONS

YOUR VOICE JOURNAL

MY DREAMS WITH AUDIO

Some of the goals of Victor's programs include

Increased awareness in body safety • Improve self-esteem • Confidence building
Overcome adversity (Resiliency) • Increase Gratitude
Learn and appreciate the art of "Kindness"

Made in the USA
Middletown, DE
10 March 2019